Date Due

Feb 4/91			
WA Feb 91			
CEN Oct 92			
JAN 28 '95			
MAR 18 '95			
JAN 06 '96			
MAY 25 '96			
FEB 20 '98			
DEC 18 1999			
JAN 08 2000			
JUN 22 2002			

BRODART, INC. Cat. No. 23 233 Printed in U.S.A.

971 .9 102 092 Ryan -B

Brennan, Ann, 1939-
The real Klondike Kate / T. Ann Brennan. --
Fredericton, N.B. : Goose Lane, c1990.
207 p. : ill., maps, ports.

Includes index.
Bibliography: p. [205]-207.
04534255 ISBN:0864921349 (pbk.)

1. Ryan, Kate, 1869-1932. 2. Pioneers - Yukon Territory - Klondike River Valley - Biography. 3. Women pioneers - Yukon Territory - Klondike River
(SEE NEXT CARD)

5753 91JAN02 06/he 1-00958840

The Real KLONDIKE KATE

T. ANN BRENNAN

Goose Lane Editions

Published with the assistance of the Canada Council and the New Brunswick Department of Tourism, Recreation & Heritage, 1990.

Photographs appearing with the abbreviation (NAC) are from the National Archives of Canada; those appearing with (HJM) are by Henry J. Woodside, reproduced courtesy of the National Archives of Canada. Photographs appearing with the credit (KMK) are from the private collection of Katherine Ryan McKernan.

The map appearing on page 38 is reproduced from *The Sinking of the Princess Sophia: Taking the North Down With Her*, by Ken Coates and Bill Morrison, ©Ken Coates and Bill Morrison (Oxford University Press Canada, 1990), reprinted by permission of the publisher. The map appearing on page 48 is reproduced from *Canadian Papers in Archaeology and History*, no. 19, with the permission of Canadian Parks Service, Environment Canada.

The photograph appearing on the cover and on page 186 is from an article by William Lewis Edmunds entitled "The Woman Called Klondike Kate," published in *Maclean's Magazine*, December 1922, courtesy of the Fisher Rare Book Library, University of Toronto, Canada.

Book design by Julie Scriver
Printed in Canada by Hignell Printing

Canadian Cataloguing in Publication Data
Brennan, T. Ann, 1939-
The real Klondike Kate

ISBN 0-86492-134-9

1. Ryan, Kate, 1869-1932. 2. Klondike River Valley (Yukon) – Gold discoveries. 3. Pioneers – Yukon Territory – Klondike River Valley – Biography. 4. Women pioneers – Yukon Territory – Klondike River Valley – Biography. I. Title.

FC4045.K56Z49 1990 971.9'102'092 C90-097662-4
F1095.K5B72 1990

Goose Lane Editions
248 Brunswick Street
Fredericton, New Brunswick
Canada E3B 1G9

The story of Katherine Ryan
is dedicated to
The People of Johnville

"He does not die who can
bequeath some influence
to the land he knows"

Johnville Memorial

Illustrations

Contents

Kate as a young girl in Johnville: "Sweet Sixteen." (KMK)

Introduction

My search for Kate Ryan began in 1958 when I arrived in Bath, New Brunswick, young and eager to take up my first teaching position. Tom Gallagher was the resident owner of my boarding house. In the latter part of his life, Tom spent most of his day seated at a command post in a rocking chair, reviewing the boarders as they came and went. He recited stories and gossiped with anyone who would listen, and as the youngest female boarder, I became his favourite audience for stories about "Klondike Kate." I never knew when he was fabricating and when he was telling the truth, but his ramblings contradicted anything I had read about the Yukon Gold Rush. When he spoke of Kate Ryan, a local girl who went to the Yukon in 1898, he insisted that "Klondike Kate" was her nickname, but he was quick to add that she was not a dance-hall girl but a heroine of the northern frontier.

At the time, I paid only polite attention to Tom, but as the years went by Katherine Ryan's life and mine continued to overlap. In the early 1970s, Major and Pat Evans returned from Whitehorse, where Major worked in the Department of Tourism, to visit our farm in Johnville. My casual remark that the homestead of "Klondike Kate" was visible from the kitchen window took Major aback. Historians in Whitehorse had been searching for Kate Ryan for years, and Major asked me to gather more information about her. Agreeing to do him this small favour started me on a quest that would obsess me for fifteen years. By this time, Tom Gallagher had died, but cousins, grandnieces and grandnephews and many others who had known the Ryan family still lived nearby. Kate's nephew actually occupied the family homestead. The whole community held its native daughter in great esteem.

One story or photo led to another and soon the pieces began to fit together. My greatest contributor was my husband's aunt, Annie Brennan Guest. Aunt Annie, a shy and humble woman born in 1892, clearly recalled the thrill of attending a tea in honour of the famous "Klondike Kate" when she had returned to Johnville for a visit. "I still remember her dress and her long sable coat," Aunt Annie said. "The dress rustled when she walked. Miss Ryan told me the rustle sounded like the Northern Lights she loved so much." Other elderly people in the community, along with Kate's relatives, contributed to my growing files: Tom Bohan, Dr. Tom Brennan, Loretta Colton, Clarence Corcoran, Francis Cullen, Bernard Davenport, and Bob and Walter Ryan. Mrs. John Lang of Glassville recounted a visit from the Reverend John Pringle to Glassville when he was Moderator of the Presbyterian Church in Canada. In his sermon, Pringle told the congregation about his missionary work in the north and his friendship with Katherine Ryan. Meanwhile, Major Evans reported that Allen Innis-Taylor and the Whitehorse Museum had transferred the early Yukon files to the National Archives in Ottawa. From then on, my holidays and business trips were always extended so I could squeeze in a few hours in Ottawa to pore over newspapers, RCMP files and historical records.

Kate's life is documented perhaps a little more fully than the lives of most of the Yukon pioneers because of her official duties, but she was, for all her bravery and good works, an ordinary person. The incidents in this book are true, but I have fleshed out Kate's story from various sources other than historical documents. Newspaper reporters sometimes quoted Kate, and I have used these quotations as well as quotations in William Lewis Edmunds's 1922 *Maclean's* article as speech. I have also turned into speech the stories told by those who knew her or remembered what others said about her. Kate's thoughts and feelings have been derived from these sources, too. Most of the words spoken by other people in this book have been taken from newspaper articles, journals, diaries, RCMP reports and similar sources. Johnville residents, their relatives and friends, people that I met in my travels, and others who wrote to me after hearing about my project sometimes gave me newspaper clippings. Never imagining that these clippings would have any but sentimental value, most of the people who saved them didn't record where or when the items were published. I used information and quoted speech from these unidentifiable sources just as I used the same kinds of material from identified publications.

Certain habits and customs have persisted in Johnville from its founding to this day, such as mixing earth from an old home with earth at a new home and hanging a blessed rosary on the clothesline to chase away rain clouds on picnic day. I have assumed that Kate did these things, even though no single document exists as "proof." I have made extensive use of RCMP records and also used the detailed journals kept by Henry Woodside to narrate Kate's experiences. For instance, Kate left for the north the last week of February, 1898, but I do not know whether she went aboard the *Tees*. I have made Henry Woodside's experiences and observations Kate's, because Woodside's journal records the voyage he made to Wrangell at about that time. If she wasn't aboard his ship, she travelled on one very much like it. The North West Mounted Police detachment left Vancouver for Wrangell on 28 February 1898 on the *Tees*, and they and Kate travelled up the frozen Stikine River as soon as they could. RCMP records tell about the Wrangell-Dewdney leg of the trip into the north. The purpose of these additions has been to show Kate's personality and character by making her adventures as vivid on the page as they were in life. Any mistakes in fact about anyone living or dead are unintentional.

In March 1981 I visited John Ryan Jr. and his daughter Katherine Ryan McKernan in Vancouver to discuss my research on Kate. They were reluctant to disclose details about Kate's life, fearing that any reference to "Klondike Kate" would only add to the shame and dishonour already attached to John's Aunt Kate by associating her again with the dance-hall girl who had claimed Kate Ryan's deeds as her own. Kit McKernan did, however, provide numerous photos from Kate's personal album. I hope they will feel now that Aunt Kate's name is cleared, and that she will never again be confused with the entertainer who adopted Katherine Ryan's past as her own.

In Vancouver, I went to Mass at Kate's church, Holy Rosary Cathedral, and I imagined that Kate was sitting in one of the pews that day. Outside, winos and prostitutes lined the street and, a country girl like Kate, I was offended. Then I looked up at the mountains and understood what Kate meant when she said, "I hunger to make my abode where the works of nature and not man abound." I am grateful for her inspiration.

Pierre Berton and Michel Tremblay both helped me hold on to the faith that I could and should complete this project. Pierre Berton supplied me with a gentle stick: after a conversation, he said, in effect, "This is your story. Go home and write it." Michel Tremblay held out a carrot. He told me and my fellow participants at a conference in Montreal in 1988, "It takes great courage to be a historian. It is very pretentious to write history and more pretentious to take history and ask the questions. Why do it then? I do it because I love it and am humble enough to try."

In a more tangible sense, I would like to thank S.W. Horrall, Historian, RCMP, Ottawa, and M.J.H. Wake, C/M, Director of RCMP Museum, Regina; Les Mobbs, National Archives, Photographic Section and A.M. Kelly, Ottawa; Susan Belyea, Valerie Brooker, Wendy Marr and the late Robert Tweedie in New Brunswick; Dick Shaw in Bangor, Maine; Gus Long and Isobel McGuire-MacLaurin in Vancouver; and Gerry Kristianson in Victoria.

In my search for Kate Ryan's story, I have been blessed by the support of many people. Jim Morrison, an experienced newspaperman, taught me to tell Kate's story with verve while remaining true to the facts. Major Evans bombarded me, not only with photos, maps, magazine clippings and references, but also with encouraging letters. I am also especially grateful to Laurel Boone, my editor, who took my rough manuscript and polished it, making us all proud of Kate's story.

But it has been my family who gave me strength to persist when I became discouraged and wanted to throw the project to the four winds. Thanks to each and every one of them, my dream of telling the story of the real Klondike Kate has come true.

Johnville

T*he warm stirrings* of an August night drifted into the small room, breathing faint wisps of cool air over the face of the mother struggling in labour. She could hear voices in the other room, on the other side of the curtain, joining in unison as the clicking of the rosary beads mingled with the murmurs of the summer night. Anne Ryan had only her belief in the Bishop's promise and the rough kindness of Ellen DeMerchant, the midwife, for comfort. Ellen hovered over her, offering encouragement. The baby would come any time now, so she prepared the aging mother for the final struggle. Silently she prayed that both Anne and her baby would survive.

At the sound of the infant's first cry, the voices of the women in the kitchen suddenly stopped. After the merest second, they raised again, now in glorious thanksgiving. Once more the Bishop and God had protected them. To Ellen's relief, the baby girl was strong and healthy in spite of the difficult birth. With the wisdom of her trade, she gave her exhausted patient firm advice that the priest in the next room could not hear — advice that would end Anne's childbearing.

Three days after the baby's birth, Father Bernard McKeany returned to the cabin to baptize her. In his clear and careful script, he recorded the details in the church ledger: "On August 23, 1869, I baptized Katherine Ryan daughter of Anne Holden and Patrick Ryan lawful parents." Baby Katherine slept peacefully through the ceremony, innocent of the knowledge that she was a member of the first generation of a new country. Little did anyone at that humble baptism know that this baby, Katherine Ryan, would become an important builder of the Canadian nation.

Father McKeany attended his flock of new Irish settlers in Johnville, New Brunswick, with love and devotion. He had just arrived from the city of Boston, where he had been ministering to his countrymen who had fled Ireland's cruel potato famine. Boston was growing explosively, and the immigrants' struggles there drove many of them further and further into the North

American vastness in search of their own land and the freedom they craved. Those who came to New Brunswick in the early years of settlement spread out all over the province, each family seeking a plot of land or a small corner where they could survive. Saint John was the port of entry for thousands of the first settlers. There they were helped by the Immigrant Aid Society, which Bishop John Sweeney had founded in 1849 to succour the desperate people flooding into the country.

In the spring of 1865, Katherine's parents came to Saint John, lured by Bishop Sweeney's promise of a hundred acres of free land. After forty miserable days in quarantine on Partridge Island, they started on the last leg of their journey to the upper reaches of the St. John River Valley. With ten other families, Pat Ryan of Donegal, his wife Anne and their five children set up housekeeping in the wilderness of New Brunswick. Four years later, when Katherine made her presence known in the Ryan household, her family owned a rather crude but solid home, and her father had constructed outbuildings so they could keep a cow and a flock of healthy sheep, which grazed on the nearby hills. Kate's eldest brother, James, was already a man of eighteen, entitled to his own 100 acres of free land. Her brother Andrew was over six feet tall, even though he had just turned sixteen. At thirteen, Margaret took complete charge of the household during her mother's last confinement. Her job included the care of the three younger children, Hannah, nine, John, five and Nora, three, all clamouring for the attention of their ailing Mother. The Ryans and their friends named their rural community Johnville, after the Bishop who had led them to this new country. Though difficult to tame, the land had a silent beauty, and survival depended on the pioneers' ability to meet nature half-way. They had to clear away the timber to make their farms, but soon, just as the Bishop had promised them, the land began to bear an abundance of food and yield a profitable harvest.

True to Irish custom, Anne had brought a small parcel of Irish soil, carefully wrapped in a towel, from her old home in Donegal. After Katherine's birth, she realized that this strange country was to be her permanent home; she would never return to her beloved Ireland. With the younger children gathered around her, she carefully mixed the soil of her native Ireland with the rich brown earth of Johnville, offering prayers to the Holy Mother that here at last her family would find peace and freedom.

The following years were bountiful for the Johnville settlers. To Anne it appeared that the soil she brought from Ireland had multiplied as the hills of Johnville became a well-tended semblance of the country they had left across the ocean. Green field crops and pastures replaced the mass of brush and timber. Smoke from the chimneys of the small cabins in the clearings floated into the clear sky. Potato fields appeared in patterned rows, dotted with rock piles that looked as if they had been dropped by an errant child.

The Ryan family was a happy family, but like all settlers they depended upon their neighbours for survival. The Johnville pioneers were united by Irish traditions and their Catholic religion. They had traded starvation and the yoke of English oppression for a life of hard work, harsh elements and a meagre existence, but their freedom and the promise of material success made it all worth while. In time, they stopped yearning for their old homes across the ocean, and their hatred of their oppressors softened to a gentle bitterness.

Bishop Sweeney was satisfied with the success of his Johnville flock, and it pleased him to keep informed of their needs and progress. When he sent word that he was about to arrive for a visitation, Johnville planned a great celebration. His travelling companion, John McGuire, M.P., recorded their arrival in Johnville:

> As we proceeded through a couple of miles of dense forest in which the dark green of the pine and the brighter verdure of the spruce contrasted with the prevailing sombre hue of the hardwood, occasionally relieved by the bright yellow leaves of the beech and the gleaming crimson of the maple — we were met by two or three of the country waggons laden with grain and driven by strapping young fellows, roughly but comfortably clad, their stout horses trotting briskly along the bishop's model highway. These young men were delighted to see their good pastor whom they saluted with a mixture of respect and affection and

> with whom they chatted with the most perfect freedom. They promised to spread far and wide the grateful intelligence that Mass would be celebrated at eight o'clock the following morning in the little chapel in the settlement.

Gathering his people in the chapel under the tall swaying pine trees for a Mass of Thanksgiving, Bishop Sweeney offered them a homily of praise and advice that was inscribed in the church records so future generations would remember the holy man and his words.

"I have staked off 100 acres for a church and school that you will one day build," he said, "so that your children and their children after will continue in the religion of our ancestors and also that they will be educated and succeed in this beautiful country." He admonished the men of the parish, "There are to be no taverns in Johnville."

Aware of the Irish weakness for drink, he made it plain that there was no time for frivolity in this country. They must work hard if they were to live and thrive. As the Bishop continued with his sermon, he could see a group of women nervously trying to get his attention. Shyly they came forward and confided to him their greatest fear.

"Beggin' your pardon, Sir," the spokeswoman said, "but Sir, we're sor' afraid of childbearing without the aid of a doctor in this wilderness."

Understanding the women's fears, he offered them the only solace he could. "No woman of Johnville will ever die in childbirth for want of a doctor," he vowed. The women went away clutching their faith in the Bishop's words. The promise was kept, and the legend remains.

Katherine Ryan grew in this prospering environment and, being the baby of the family, she was the apple of her father's eye. Kate, as her brothers called her, soon became part of the family work system. Even a child of four could set the table and pick potatoes; there were plenty of jobs for little hands as well as for big ones.

Pat Ryan was not an ambitious man. Always following some wild scheme or another, he left the farm work to his dutiful wife and their sons. Pat's first business venture was a grocery store. It seemed to him that there would be more money in groceries than in farming, and — he hoped — a lot less work. He cleared the family's possessions out of the front room of their cabin at the top of Campbell Hill, built a rough lean-to on the back for a kitchen, and set up shop. He soon earned a reputation for squeezing the pennies so hard, sweat would drop off of them. But his patient wife could always be depended upon to add an extra sweet for the little one or give credit when Pat was away for the day. The store became a gathering place for entertainment and for trade in gossip as well as goods. Kate grew up unnoticed, playing among the barrels and boxes. The wood stove's tang mingled with the sweet smell of the sticky molasses kegs. During the winter, the air would be tinged with the pungent smelt of potatoes stored in the earth cellar under the floor. In the evenings, Pat cleared the counter for the card games that the men played with the seriousness of Russian roulette. The monotonous snap of the cards and the hand thumping continued into the night. The pennies pushed back and forth across the counter were finally gathered by the lucky winner, only to reappear the next night and go home in some other man's pocket.

Before long, Pat tired of the store and soon left most of the business to his wife and children while he went off looking for a new adventure. By chance and Moses Brennan, he found his next profession. Moses had come to Johnville with his new wife Bridget via Boston from County Carlow, Ireland. After several years of hardships and struggle, Moses and Bridget had received a grant of land on the next tier over from the Ryan farm. In a few short years, Moses had become a leading citizen of the community, having built a frame house, established himself as a finish carpenter and prospered as a farmer. Moses was also one of the first in the settlement to own a horse. Pat Ryan happened to visit Moses the day the mare kicked young Willie Brennan. Moses, terrified that his son would die, went furiously for his gun. Pat finally persuaded the angry father that a horse was just too valuable an animal to shoot. By this time, little Willie was coming around. When Moses saw he would not die, he began to calm down. As a good neighbour, Pat volunteered to take the disreputable animal off his hands, with, of course, a small sum of money to boot. Before Moses could regain his composure enough to change his mind, Pat had set off for home with his first horse.

Kate could not believe her eyes. She had prayed for a horse for as long as she could remember, and now, here was her father leading the most wonderful animal she could possibly imagine. What did it matter that the horse came to them in disgrace? A horse was a horse, and she begged her father for the first ride. Realizing his children's intentions, he gave them their first lesson in the horse trade.

"Never, never stand behind a horse," he cautioned, as he led the chestnut mare to the back hovel. "A horse is not a pet," he went on, trying to convince the breathless children that this wonderful animal was a dangerous creature. Pat continued his lesson, scolding them and warning them against this particular lady and her bad habits.

"You must first understand the horse and control it. Never let the horse control you, or all is lost. Is that understood, Katie, my lass?"

"Oh, yes. Now, Father, may I ride her, please?

Before Pat could restrain her, Kate climbed up on the big work horse. Animal and child, grateful to be free of farm chores, sauntered off to explore the hills of Johnville.

Looking back years later, Kate remembered that summer as the most wonderful of her childhood. She would never forget the glorious warm evenings when she wandered over the hills with the skittish mare, looking out over the river valley opening below her. She knew she was one of the luckiest girls in the world. But before harvest time, the mare was up to her old tricks. Despite Kate's tears and pleas, she was traded for the gentler Queenie. In September, both Queenie and Kate had to go to work, and there was no more time for fun. Man, woman, child and beast slaved from daylight to dark harvesting the potatoes. But after the harvest, Pat and the boys added more room to the hovel, which now began to take the shape of a real barn. Soon three more horses joined Queenie, and horse trading became a family occupation that would span four generations.

Fulfilling Bishop Sweeney's plan, the Johnville settlers built a one room school, nestled on the side of the Carlow hill and sheltered from the wind by tall firs. The teacher planted a rose bush the first spring, and it soon offered up blooms in the summer and, in the winter, round red rose hips to make into stringers for the Christmas concert. Reading and writing delighted Kate and her sister Nora. Their parents considered it a wonderful gift to have an educated child in the family, but they did not encourage the older boys to attend school after the first few years. Once they were old enough they spent the winter in the woods with the men, and in spring and fall they worked in the fields. But for Kate school was glorious. There she read stories of places far away, stories of grand cities and countries that lay beyond the St. John River. School awakened in Kate a zest for knowledge about people and places she had never known existed.

Kate's childhood flew by. Each spring brought release from the isolation and hardship of the long winter months. For the women and children, winter could be desolate, because the men and older boys worked in the woods all winter and did not emerge until spring break-up. The women and children cared for the farm animals alone, and had only each other to depend on in sickness and emergencies. But spring also brought a complete rebirth of the land. A child of the forest, Kate watched the April rains bring out the small tight buds on the poplar trees, and she jumped across the Ryans' small stream as it cracked its winter shell of ice and overflowed its bank. On the hill behind the horse barn, her father's sheep cropped the new grass with complete freedom. Kate searched the hills for the first hint of trilliums and violets. Where the fields met the woods, the colours changed as the snows melted and left in their wake the greens mixed with the soft colours of early life. As the ice receded from the nearby Shiktehawk Stream, it uncovered the first fiddleheads, fern shoots shaped like the scroll of a violin, nature's earliest contribution to the Ryan table. Anne would shoo her daughters off to pick the first pailful, and the girls were so eager for their father's praise that they needed no coaxing to run off in search of the river delicacies.

As the corn and hay shot up the summer Kate turned fourteen, so did Kate. The neighbours' constant comments on her stature embarrassed her, and even the new parish priest, Father

William Chapman, remarked on her growth. She tried hunching her shoulders, hoping no one would notice she was as tall as her brother John. It did not seem to help. When she hunched over, her mother would swat her back and tell her to straighten up before she became a hunchback. That fate seemed far worse than being tall, so she and Nora began to practice being ladies of note as they walked the beams in the barn.

When the boys came of age, they were not long leaving the nest to make places for themselves in the world. There were great opportunities in America and the Canadian west, new beginnings and distant places that needed lads with strong arms ready to do a day's work. James moved to Minneapolis, and John, rumour had it, was courting a girl from downriver. Margaret married Patrick Colten and together they moved to their own homestead. Only Nora, John and Kate remained at home. Johnville now had a post office, a resident doctor and new roads. The daily train from Saint John to Edmundston passed through the nearby village of Bath. Kate was never at a loss for work — there were never enough hours in the day to do all her farm work and the community social work that needed to be done. Springs came and went, and in spite of questions from family and friends, Kate made no plans for the future. Perhaps she was destined to remain at home and take care of her parents. But as the days turned into years, she continually asked herself what lay ahead for her.

Three days before Kate's twenty-second birthday, the August sunrise sent silver waves across the water of the St. John River. In the pasture behind the house, the new hay barn spilled its golden wealth from the loft, and the gurgle of the brook urged Kate to get up. Her mother's call drew her reluctantly out of bed. Splashing cool water from the earthen pitcher on her face, she examined herself in the mirror. The tall thin figure of her youth had blossomed. She now stood over six feet tall in her stocking feet, and her strong build was graceful. Her blonde curls had turned light auburn, and now she smoothed her hair tightly back from face and plaited it into one thick braid. No matter how hard she tried to keep it neat, wisps of fine curls sneaked out around her face. She put on her work dress and a fresh apron, ready to face the morning chores. And there were many on this, the most special day of the summer — Picnic Day.

In Johnville, time revolved around the social event of the year, the church picnic. Tradition decreed that the picnic be held in August, and because the custom had grown ever since the settlement began, the picnic attained such importance that all personal plans, including marriages, births and even deaths were postponed until "after the picnic." The picnic was a mystical, magical event, a time to be free of work in the fields, a time to visit with friends and neighbors, exchange stories, gossip and laugh. It was the last chance for revelry before the serious time of harvest and the long winter months of isolation. Year by year after the first picnic, legends and stories about the day accumulated. Each year, the parishioners fervently repeated Bishop John Sweeney's own words: "Picnic Day will never be cancelled because of rain." Anyone who saw the slightest sign of the tiniest cloud would dash to hang a blessed rosary on the nearest clothesline, a precaution that always drove away the rain. Those of little faith coming to Johnville for the first time were always wary of such superstitions and scoffed at the silly stories and legends that were repeated every year. Yet one by one they would be drawn into the celebrations and the rekindling of the Celtic lore of the Irish.

Kate had been very much involved in the preparations for this particular picnic, one of the most ambitious socials ever organized in the whole of Carleton County. Committee members Henry Corcoran and Charles E. Gallagher had negotiated with the railway for an excursion train to come from the town of Woodstock for the day's events. Charles Gallagher, one of the most prominent businessmen in the village of Bath, had just finished a new warehouse and potato-loading shed opposite the Bath train station. The committee hastily converted these buildings into a dining hall and dance floor for the picnic. In the adjacent field, at a frolic on the preceding Sunday, the men had built booths out of rough lumber to house the games of chance and the ice cream and soda pop stands.

When Kate arrived at Gallagher Field early in the forenoon, she stepped into the midst of a commotion. The older boys helped Elias Shepherd put his swing together, and someone roped off a large circle for the pony rides. Moses Brennan brought thirty coarse jute sacks for the potato sack races. Small children darted in and out around the booths, annoying the men trying to finish setting up the games and concessions until the men scolded them, chasing them away with the warning that there would be no soda pop for naughty children. The Catholic Women's League laid out fancy work, knitted mitts and socks and jars of sweet berries in the large tent they had borrowed for their sale. The women were intent on festooning the booths and loading sheds with bunting and summer flowers when Henry Corcoran appeared with a wagon full of cedar boughs. The women added the cedar to their decorations to give the buildings the final touch of elegance, and the cedar's fresh aroma filled the air with the scent of the forest.

Everyone called the same greeting: "Great day for the picnic." Then, just to be sure, they would cast a weather eye towards the sky to make sure it was still blue and betrayed no sign of ominous clouds in the distance. The same blue sky reigned over Woodstock and enticed two hundred people to gather at the station. The train, anxious to be on its way upriver, blew out great billows of steam. The parish priest, some local singers and — dressed in their best uniforms for the special occasion — the town band met the Woodstock citizens piling aboard the train. Just as the train was about to depart, the local politicians, seizing the opportunity to meet the country folk, joined the crowd. They could not pass up a gathering of so many eligible voters so close to the fall election. As the train left the Woodstock station, the band struck up, and the merrymakers were off for Bath and the great picnic.

Mingling with the crowd in the early afternoon, Kate exulted in the number of people who had turned out for the day's celebrations. Henry Corcoran ran over to her and reported, "Kate, we've just sold our two thousandth ticket at the gate. Can you believe it? Two thousand people at the Johnville Picnic?" Never had there been such a gathering in the community. But success brought added responsibilities. Kate hurried over to the warehouse to alert the women preparing the evening meal. The warehouse had been dramatically converted into a grand dining hall in a few short hours. Long tables spread with gleaming white cloths were trimmed with festive green bows and, as centrepieces, glass jars filled with black-eyed Susans, Queen Anne's lace and other wild flowers of August. The tables groaned under the platters of chicken, the salads and the crocks of beanhole beans. To complete the menu, the tables bore the ultimate dessert, raspberry pie. Looking over the tables, Kate could only hope there would be enough to go around, for it was indeed a feast fit for a king.

Shortly before four o'clock, the revellers began to form lines and for 25¢ they ate to their hearts content. As the last sitting rose from the supper table, the sun slowly descended behind the hills, leaving an orange and fuschia wake on the peaceful river. The cries of the night hawks mingled with the strains of the fiddler tuning his violin. When the sun had left the western sky, the first couples began to drift onto the dance floor. Slowly and methodically, men and women found partners for the ballads and waltzes. To Kate's surprise, Simon Gallagher came over and asked her for a dance. He was a tall, quiet young man whom she had known all her life, just as she knew everyone in the community. But because he was the son of the prosperous Gallagher family, she did not think that he had ever noticed her. Kate proudly reached for Simon's hand and stepped on to the dance floor, ignoring her brothers' grins and glances. The night's jollity grew and the men's steps lightened as they made frequent trips outside for "a wee drap of the craeture" to quench the thirst brought on by the warm evening and the feverish dancing.

Simon returned again and again to dance with Kate, and as they joined hands for the grand circle the music soared to the rafters. The fiddler mixed the old ballads of Ireland with the jigs and reels of the new country, but only once could he be coaxed to pick up the bodhran and play "Brian Boru's March." The sound of the ancient song brought Irish settlers to their feet in a wild frenzy as they cheered the musicians on. But as the night came to a close, the music slowly grew softer. The fiddler played the good night waltz and the train whistle called the travellers to the waiting train. Reluctantly they gathered sleeping children, baskets of leftover food and treasured prizes, and boarded the train to return to Woodstock. Those who remained drifted off to their wagons for their homeward journey.

In the small hours of the morning, snuggled in the security of her cosy bed, Kate relived the excitement of the day and dreamed of the handsome young man. "It surely was the day of the Great Picnic," she mused to herself. Before sleep overtook her, she also realized that, for the first time in her life, she knew the pain of love.

Going West

T*he harvest of 1892* was the best anyone in the St. John Valley could remember. Potatoes filled every root cellar and potato house. Children followed behind anxious farmers, who unearthed their valuable crop with large forks. The children scooped the potatoes into baskets and lugged them to the barrels that stood waiting to be filled. For the new farmers, it was a joy beyond comprehension to see such a rich abundance from the land. The harvest meant not only food for their families but cash as well. At the Ryan farm, Kate had little time for social life. She put away her romantic ideas and went to work in the fields with her father and brothers. Simon Gallagher did not return to college that fall but started to work in his father's store. During the months after harvest, the tall young man and Kate stepped out together to all the social gatherings, so much so that the community started to consider them a couple. Kate tried to ignore her friends' remarks and her family's teasing, laughing at their comments and keeping her thoughts to herself. She refused to take part in her family's speculations about her future as Mrs. Simon Gallagher, but silently she dreamed her own dreams.

The August picnic had capped the Johnville parish building fund, and that fall the congregation united in a flurry of building. A last tremendous push finished the Church of St. John the Evangelist in time for Midnight Mass on Christmas Eve. Kate, Nora and the other ladies trimmed the church with fir and pine boughs and whatever bright bits of colour their homes would yield, preparing to worship God in the beauty of holiness at this first special Mass in their new church. Early on Christmas Eve night, Kate's father brought the horses around to the front of the house. He had filled the sled box with sweet clean hay from the barn and covered it with heavy horse blankets. The horses snorted their greetings as they pawed the snow, impatient to begin their journey. Off they flew, harness bells jingling, down the hill and up the next to Crains' Corner. There, neighbours shouted greetings and added their own bells to the music of the night. As the merry sounds carried over the hills through the frosty air, the horses, caught up in the excitement, quickened their pace.

Near the top of Johnville hill, Kate peeped from under the horse blankets in the sled to see the lights of the church in the distance. She heard the steeple bell echoing over the hills for the first time. The moon shone crisp and cold on the silver snow as the hills throughout the valley resounded with the music of the new bell. Inside the warm church, nave and sanctuary blazed with long tallow candles that cast flickering shadows against the high arches. Kate had never seen such a magnificent sight in all her life. The garlands of greenery that she and Nora and their friends had worked so hard to make draped the front of the high altar and adorned the window sills. Smaller branches, tied with red cotton bows and accented with pine cones and red berries, decked walls and pews. The air was tense with excitement as each family filed into its own special place. Each family had bought a pew, so everyone had a special seat; anyone who presumed to sit in someone else's place would have been soundly reprimanded.

When Father Chapman entered the sanctuary, the congregation stood in unison to begin the mass. Kate could hardly keep her mind on the Latin as her eyes followed the shadows on the walls, walls newly painted a bright white and trimmed with gold leaf and the delicate blue of the Blessed Virgin. The tiny choir intoned the Latin chants as the priest swung the thurible, adding the pungent odour of incense to the sweet exhalations of the festive fir and cedar. The Gallagher family occupied its designated pew ahead of the Ryans. Simon's mother sat tall and erect. Her new fur coat was the most elegant ever seen in Johnville, and her hat drew furtive glances of envy from all the women behind her. Simon, tall and handsome next to his mother, did not turn around. Watching him, Kate felt a tightening in her throat. She had fallen deeply in love with Simon, but all she could do was offer up fervent prayers that he felt the same for her and that her future with him would be secure.

At the Gospel proclamation, Father Chapman dressed in his handsome crimson chasuble, stepped up into his pulpit and smiled warmly at his congregation. He was overcome with pride, pride in his new church and pride in the people seated in front of him. In a few short years these hardy souls had cleared the forest, planted crops, built homes and created a community. Now, they had completed this glorious monument in thanksgiving to God. Father Chapman's voice filled with emotion as he spoke of their beloved Ireland, the land they had left just a few years ago. He reminded them of the traditions of their homeland and the faith of their ancestors.

"And now," he concluded, "you have carried the faith of your ancestors to this new land. In return, the land has given you a great deal. You are Canadians now; never forget the past but always build for the future. The future for your children is secure in this country, because it is, indeed, going to be a great country. Go in peace."

Mothers wiped tears from their eyes and held little ones close to their breasts. The priest's words sounded familiar to Kate, for her parents often reminded her of her heritage and of how important it was that she was a Canadian. She took Father Chapman's words carefully into her heart, filled with pride and knowing that at least in some small way she would contribute to this country that had given her family and community so much.

When the Mass ended, young and old alike gathered outside on the church steps. The men went off to prepare their teams as relatives and friends exchanged their gifts and greetings. Simon shyly broke away from his family and came over to Kate. He pressed a small parcel into her hand. With a smile, she concealed the package in her pocket and said nothing to her mother or Nora on the journey home. Her heart flew up to the vibrant moon as the sleigh bells echoed her joy at the wonders of love. Not until she gained the privacy of her own bedroom did she remove the box from the bright paper. In a burgundy velvet case lay a delicate filigree cameo necklace with three exquisite seed pearl drops. She held the box close to her heart and a tear trickled down her cheek.

On Christmas morning, after the boys went outside to do

chores, she brought the necklace from its resting place to show her mother.

"Ah, 'tis beautiful, Katie," Anne exclaimed. "Surely the finest necklace I have ever seen, but oh, dear, the pearls are surely a sign of the tears you will shed for this man."

Kate laughed at her mother's superstitions. This necklace assured Kate that Simon loved her as much as she loved him, and she would not listen to her mothers silly, old-fashioned sayings.

The seasons came and went. Winter gave way to spring and finally summer returned. Kate and Simon, the courting couple, attended all the dances and socials together, but Kate did not ask Simon his intentions, and he did not offer to tell her. Content in her world, she waited patiently for what seemed to be the inevitable. Nora married and moved to Bangor, Maine, causing a great upheaval in the Ryan household because her chosen husband did not meet with family approval. But Kate showed her joy for her sister by acting as a witness to the marriage. She hoped that Nora would find happiness. At least she had moved away from the farm to lead a life of her own, something Kate so far could only dream about. The weight of the family was beginning to bear heavily on her, and she longed for a home and an identity.

Once again, picnic day drew near. In the hope of repeating last year's success, the committee decided to hold it again at the Gallagher field in Bath. Once more, a train was hired for the trip from Woodstock, and once more the committee organized the greatest day of the year. They cleared the last potatoes out of the Gallagher warehouses, swept them down, and scrubbed and furnished them for the supper and dance.

The great day itself was another success for the parish, even though not quite so many people had turned out. Kate was cutting pies when Simon came to the back door of the warehouse dining hall and asked her to go for a walk along the river. His presence and attention made her flush, but she called her cousin Rose to take her place at the pie table and removed her apron to join him. In the warehouse dance hall, the orchestra tuned their instruments for the dance. Simon took Kate's hand and drew her away from the crowd to the privacy of the river bank. The evening shadows lengthened as she waited for him to speak, trying to suppress the pounding of her heart and not wanting him to see her feelings. He touched her gently on the arm and she turned to face him.

"Katie, I've something serious I must discuss with you," he began.

She acknowledged his words but her mouth went dry. The tone of his voice was not at all what she had expected.

"We've been seeing a lot of each other this past year and I am very fond of you, Kate, but . . . " Simon paused and stumbled for words that just would not come.

"Oh, damn, Katie, I've been accepted to the seminary, and Mama wants me to go back to college and enter the priesthood."

There, he finally had to courage to say it, it was done!

The words struck Kate like a thunderbolt. She had no inkling that this was what he had on his mind. She had hoped . . . but no . . . she had heard him correctly.

"I really want you, of all people, to understand," Simon added, apparently oblivious to her shock and pain. "I'm not sure if I really want to enter the priesthood, but I had to promise Mama I would go for a year. Do you understand Kate?" he pleaded as he reached for her hand.

She drew back vehemently. Oh, she understood all right. She knew the Gallaghers' prejudices against her. Gossip said that Mama Gallagher had stated flatly, "No son of mine will ever marry a poor Ryan." Kate's dreams had been clouded by the belief that Simon would not let his mother stand in the way of their love. But she knew now that it was hopeless to offer words in defence. Simon was not the man she had thought he was. The hand controlling the Gallagher lives and tenaciously gripping the purse strings ruled over matters of the heart, too. She, Kate Ryan, a poor girl from "out back," did not measure up to the family's expectations. Pat Ryan's daughter would never be good enough for the Gallaghers, Mama had seen to that. Anger and hurt raced through her mind, but she cut them short and abruptly faced Simon.

"Yes, it's a great thing you're doing, Simon. I do wish you well. I am glad for this opportunity to speak to you. I will be leaving Johnville myself after harvest. It's to the great west I'm going." Kate had no idea why she offered the lie, but the look on Simon's face made her glad that she had.

"You remember mother's cousin, Mary Haley? Why, she has written asking me to go to work for her in Seattle, and I'll be leaving right after digging."

This lie was a half-truth. Mary had written some months ago, but she had not sent for Kate, she had sent for her cousin Rose. In that instant, however, Kate made a decision that would change her life. She, not Rose, would go to Seattle. In her heart, she knew she did not deserve the prejudice and snobbery of the Gallagher family, and was determined that she would make a name for herself so that one day they would realize that she was someone special. At the moment, though, the hurt overwhelmed her and she could no longer control her tears. She turned and left Simon standing on the river bank. Crossing the fair grounds towards her father's wagon, she could hear the strains of "Brian Boru's March," and she vowed to her ancestors that she would never forgive Simon Gallagher.

Kate kept her word. But her spirits sagged on the bleak October day on which she left her country home to travel across the continent to Seattle. Since Simon had admitted that he was going to the seminary, Kate had steeled herself for a future without him. There was nothing for her in New Brunswick except heartbreak. Time had begun its slow healing as she began to look forward to her trip and the future it promised. Seattle would be much more exciting than a marriage in Johnville, she was sure she was making the right decision, and yet, as she prepared to board the train at the Bath station, she felt certain that her heart would break. With one foot on the steel steps of the train, she hesitated. Her wise mother reached out and supported her, pushing her forward toward the dreams she knew she herself could never attain.

"Go Katie," she said. "Here is your chance to see the world. You must try your wings and learn to fly."

Just as the train began its journey through the valley of the St. John, the sun broke through the clouds, illuminating the brilliant fall hills. The beauty of the landscape and the excitement of the passing villages and towns soon eased the tears and the tightness in Kate's throat. Finally, her emotions in full control, she settled back in her seat and began to think about the journey she had just begun.

Friends and relatives acted as stepping stones for Kate as she travelled across the continent. First, she and Nora enjoyed a grand week-long reunion in Bangor. Kate almost gave in to Nora's pleas to stop and settle in Bangor, but some unknown force drew her onward — not just the prospect of a new job, but her growing sense of adventure. Before she left Johnville, she had known no other life. She had known nothing of the great world, and now she was meeting it face to face every day. There were places to see, people to meet, experiences to share. Contrary to her father's stern warning to be wary of strangers, she found her politeness and her friendly attitude returned. She just couldn't stop in Bangor. She just couldn't give up her life of freedom, her new independence. Never a day went by that she did not remember her mother's words: "Don't look back, Kate."

From Bangor she travelled west to visit her brother James in Minneapolis. It had been many years since they had seen each other, and she was a welcome guest in his home. She brought with her gifts and news of family and friends. It was a relief for her to see her elder brother succeeding as a Minneapolis city policeman with tall, strapping young boys of his own. But she was too eager to reach her destination to linger long in Minneapolis. She longed to see Seattle for herself, this new city bursting at the seams with trade and industry.

Seattle was one of the most important seaports on the Pacific coast and, after all, the sea was the life line to the world. The streets teemed with people from all corners of the globe. In Johnville, Kate had only heard about people with different coloured skins, but in Seattle she met people of all nationalities. At the Haley home, Kate took charge of the large household. Mary's husband Pat, a contractor and builder, travelled constantly to supervise his projects. Mary suffered from endless bouts of phlebitis in her legs, a result of her many pregnancies. When her illness confined her to bed, she left her bustling household and six young children under Kate's supervision. Not only that, but a stream of business associates, relatives and friends dropped in for meals or overnight visits. Kate was busy.

Kate in Vancouver, 1898. (KMK)

By the spring of 1894, Mary's legs had improved, and she had added a young Irish immigrant girl to her household. She urged Kate to apply for a job offered by the Sisters at the Nahomish Hospital. The Sisters needed to recruit young ladies to train in hospital work. Trained nurses were rare, and they jumped at the chance to hire a Catholic girl with Kate's qualifications. Nursing came naturally to Kate, and her generosity, optimism and strong physique made her a favourite with the patients as well as with the nuns. Under their careful guidance, Kate learned a great deal about the practice of medicine. She read every book she could, watched the doctors carefully and was not afraid to ask questions. She remained at the Nahomish for two years. By the end of that time, she was a confident trained nurse.

But the wanderlust Kate found she had inherited from her father would not subside. One day, she received a letter from Moses Brennan, Jr. and his new wife Lou. Promises of free land, adventure and wealth had lured Moses and Lou to Vancouver. Before long, Kate, too, succumbed to the blandishments of the "Province of Promise." In Vancouver, she happily rejoined the many friends and relatives who had been drawn into the migration to new frontier. The Johnville contingent included Henry Corcoran, George Ryan and Pat Brennan, all seeking their fortune. As soon as Kate arrived in Vancouver, she began nursing at the hospital. For awhile, she was content amidst the excitement of a new city being born. Vancouver was neither as developed nor as genteel as Victoria, across the Strait, but Kate found in Vancouver the opportunity she needed. Not only did she have a good job and friends around her, but the mountains that overlooked and protected the city of Vancouver fascinated her. Their presence drew her forward like a magnet. She would sit and meditate, letting her thoughts run idly around her head, until she began to imagine that the mountains controlled her life. Her mind filled with questions: What lay beyond the mountains? What secrets did they hold? Were they her destiny? She had learned in Seattle that she would never be content living in a large city. She missed the countryside and the woods of New Brunswick, and now she became obsessed with the desire to live where God and nature were supreme.

Late in the summer of 1897, the Almighty seemed to answer Kate's prayers personally. In a small unknown creek, hundreds of miles from the Vancouver sidewalks, three men made a discovery that would change Kate's life and alter the history of Canada.

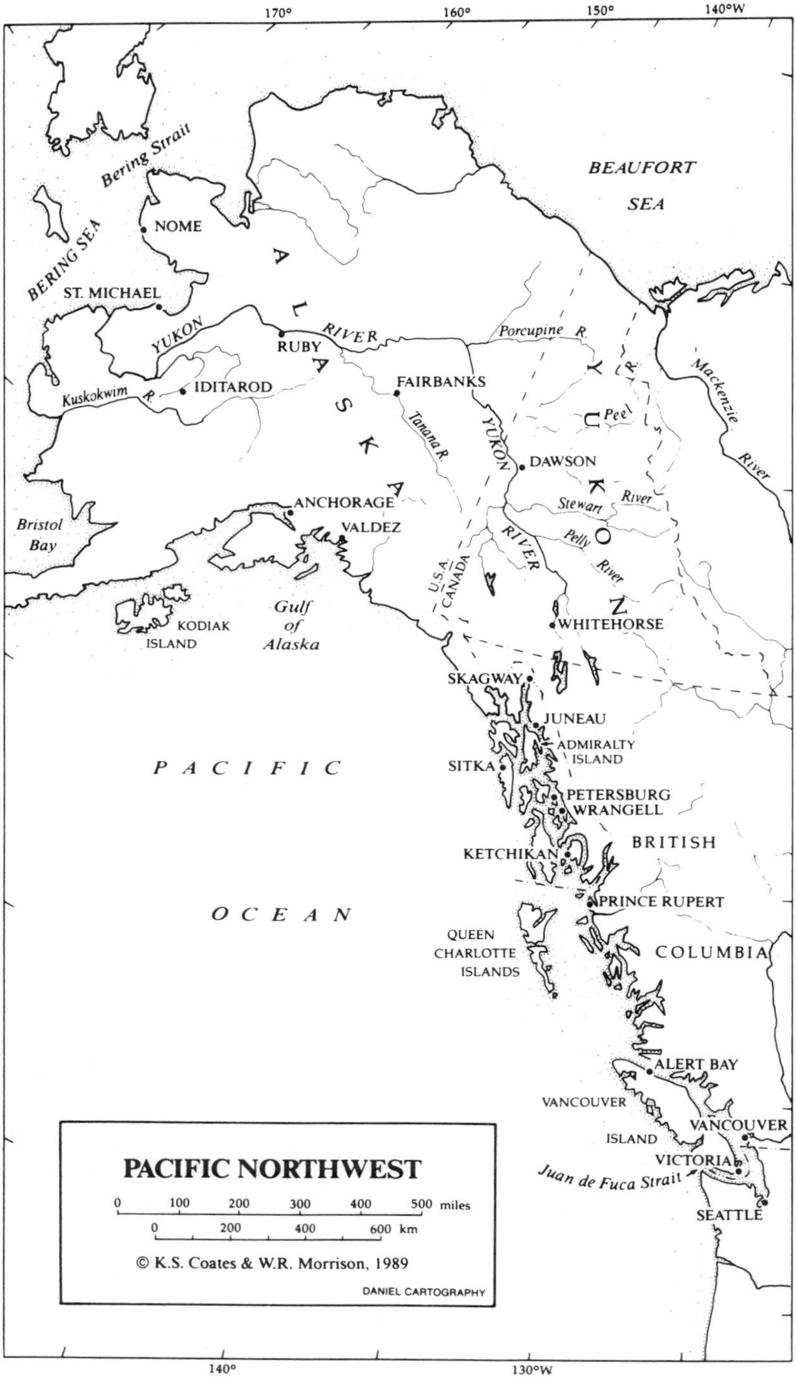
170°
160°
150°
140°W
75°
70°
65°
60°
55°
50°
45° N
140°
130°W
Bering Strait
BERING SEA
NOME
ST. MICHAEL
YUKON
RUBY
RIVER
ALASKA
BEAUFORT
SEA
Porcupine R.
Mackenzie River
Peel R.
YUKON
FAIRBANKS
IDITAROD
Kuskokwim R.
Tanana R.
DAWSON
Stewart River
Pelly River
RIVER
ANCHORAGE
VALDEZ
Bristol Bay
U.S.A.
CANADA
KODIAK ISLAND
Gulf of Alaska
WHITEHORSE
SKAGWAY
JUNEAU
ADMIRALTY ISLAND
SITKA
PACIFIC
OCEAN
PETERSBURG
WRANGELL
BRITISH
KETCHIKAN
PRINCE RUPERT
QUEEN CHARLOTTE ISLANDS
COLUMBIA
ALERT BAY
VANCOUVER
ISLAND
VANCOUVER
VICTORIA
Juan de Fuca Strait
SEATTLE
PACIFIC NORTHWEST
0 100 200 300 400 500 miles
0 200 400 600 km
© K.S. Coates & W.R. Morrison, 1989
DANIEL CARTOGRAPHY

Vancouver, 1897

K*ate always remembered* the fateful day that changed her life. Up early, she set off on her usual walk to the hospital. The heat seemed intense in spite of the early hour. Vancouver had endured temperatures in the high 90's for over two weeks, and as Kate crossed Robson Street and started down the other side she felt the heat smothering the city. She had a strange sense of excitement, as if something was about to happen.

Lighthearted, she greeted familiar faces. Near the corner, the milk man and the newspaper boy were absorbed in a serious discussion. They called to her as she came within shouting distance.

"Look at this, Miss," the paperboy called. "Gold, they've found gold in the Yukon!"

There it was in bold headlines: "Gold In The Yukon." She leaned intently over the mens' shoulders, and there in the Vancouver *Sun* was the news she had been waiting for all her life. Bob Henderson, an experienced prospector, had told George Carmack he might find gold in Rabbit Creek, a tributary of the Klondike River. With his fishing partners and brothers-in-law Skookum Jim and Taglish Charlie, Carmack had searched the gravel creek bed. On August 17, 1896, the three found gold, the largest gold strike in North America. Right away, nearby prospectors staked claims from one end of the renamed Bonanza Creek to the other, up and down Eldorado Creek, and along the Klondike River. But word of this fabulous discovery didn't reach the outside world until eleven months later, when the steamers *Portland* and *Excelsior* docked in Seattle carrying the solid gold proof of the immense wealth that lay hidden in the north. Men went wild. The Seattle *Post-Intelligencer* broke the news, and Kate's Vancouver paper relayed the story of the "ton of gold."

Kate could hardly control her own excitement and almost decided not to go to work. But, forcing reason to overcome emotion, she continued her walk to the hospital, while the city came alive with people repeating the sensational news. Hawkers screamed the headlines as men and women tumbled from their beds to see what the hubbub was all about. Men in their offices pored over the papers. Housewives, delivery men and policemen all repeated the news: "Gold! They've found gold in the Yukon!" The rumours were true. Here was the chance of a lifetime, a chance to get rich, a dream come true! Here was a chance to escape the humdrum of everyday life, a chance for freedom and adventure! And everyone would make a fortune. Gold fever had struck.

Vancouver exploded with the news. Everywhere Kate turned, people in groups exchanged the last bit of news, true or false. Questions and rumours flew: Who was going? Who had already left for the north? Nuggets the size of eggs lay in the creek beds, waiting for Vancouver tradesmen, politicians, clerks and bakers to pick them up. Wealth beyond the dreams of avarice belonged to anyone with the courage to go and get it. No one had the inclination to ask, Where *is* the Yukon, anyway? or How far is it to Bonanza Creek?

From that early morning in July, the city of Vancouver began to emerge from the plodding life of a colonial seaport to one exploding with trade, finance and industry. Men and women paraded the streets in every imaginable kind of suit and costume. Bearded men in heavy hobnailed boots decked themselves in dazzling yellow Mackintosh suits. Cowboy hats, the fashion of the day, ranged in colour from subdued greys to flamboyant greens and yellows. The ultimate in style was the "Klondike Dandy," a costume consisting of a chic reversible corduroy suit accented with the most modern northern footwear, yellow-tanned waterproof boots. Man and boots could be spotted easily two blocks distant. The ladies, not to be left out, rubbed elbows with roughly-clad woodsmen as they all marched in and out of the outfitting stores newly established at prime business locations.

These outfitters offered everything that was needed, likely to be needed, or not needed at all by the smart Yukon traveller. Every merchant was an immediate expert on Yukon climate, geography, topography and rumour. Stores overflowed with fur coats, sheepskin-lined boots, trousers with fur-lined seats, sleeping bags, a mixture of miner's tools and every variety of rifle and gun. The stores themselves were an adventure. People roamed in and out exclaiming over the technological wonders of the modern equipment, all of it, of course, absolutely necessary for any venture into the Canadian north. Kate never thought for a moment about making a decision. She knew she would go north. The only question was, When?

The first northern adventurers were mostly Americans who climbed on board the *Portland* and the *Excelsior* for their return voyage. Immediately, a flotilla of rusted and worn sailing ships, steamers and fishing boats followed up the coast. Kate gave the hospital several months' notice, because she needed time to organize her adventure and save enough money for her passage. Some of her friends shared her excitement and encouraged her plans, while others told her she had lost her sanity. But she was in good company — the whole world had done that in the last few days.

As the would-be prospectors and adventurers dealt with the everyday problems of purchasing an outfit and trying to determine the easiest and cheapest route to the Yukon, their respective governments had far greater decisions to make. The boom caused grave economic trade concerns between the American business communities and their Canadian counterparts. Seattle and San Francisco began a trade war with Victoria and Vancouver, all competing for this lucrative supply market. Governments were soon involved in the arguments, and instant laws made it advantageous to buy outfits both in the United States and Canada. Extra customs duties, freight tariffs and initial tariffs compounded the problem so that prospective travellers, as one of them remarked, were "Damned by the Canadian Customs if you buy an American outfit and persecuted by the American officials if you don't."

The Yukon Gold Rush had turned the thoughts of President Theodore Roosevelt to the long-forgotten unsettled Alaskan boundary dispute. The news of the discovery of gold at an unknown frontier made settlement of the boundary question essential, immediately and on his own terms. In Canada, Prime Minister Wilfrid Laurier was equally determined to enforce ownership of land that rightfully belonged to his growing nation. The complexity of the Yukon Gold Rush for Canada was compounded by the sudden influx of thousands of people into the wild Canadian interior. Laurier immediately dispatched his most able western minister, Clifford Sifton, to develop a strategy for managing this crisis.

Sifton and his staff had a daily list of emergencies with which they had to deal, and at the same time they tried to accomplish their three most important tasks. First, they had to appoint officials to maintain law and order; second, they had to set up customs inspection posts at border points to prevent American encroachment on Canadian sovereignty; third, they had to find a way to transport Canadian goods and travellers through Canadian territory. Sifton's surveyor was James Callbreath, a native of Glenora, a trading post on the Stikine River. Callbreath knew the river and the topography of the interior thoroughly. After a summer of exploration and surveying the Stikine Valley up to Telegraph Creek and from Telegraph Creek overland 150 miles to Teslin Lake, he submitted a lengthy report to Sifton. On the basis of this report, Sifton was convinced that the only possible route to the Klondike Gold Fields would be up the Stikine River, which offered good water for steam navigation, through the British Columbia interior to Teslin Lake, across the lake and overland to the chain of lakes draining into the Yukon River. Unfortunately, there was no way to bypass Wrangell, Alaska, at the mouth of the Stikine, as the seaport landing, because the Canadian boundary was approximately forty miles upstream from Wrangell. Sifton proposed that the route be supported by a railway line over the land leg of the trip between Telegraph Creek and Teslin Lake. This railroad would be fed by a complete steamer service on the Stikine River from Wrangell to Telegraph Creek, and steamers would be built on Teslin Lake to carry people and supplies over that stretch of the route. It would be a herculean task, but Sifton believed it had to be done. He returned to Ottawa to convince his parliamentary associates that this dream could and must be achieved.

Canadian newspapers rallied to support Sifton's proposal as the only logical route for patriotic Canadians. Their argument received support from the many travellers who had already suffered at the hands of desperados and thieves in the American towns along the Alaskan Panhandle. The morality of the American West had transposed itself to the hordes that headed north to search for gold, but the code of the Wild West offended the standards of Canadians used to the British code of law and order. Canadians in the west depended on the security provided by the North West Mounted Police force, and those who headed to the Yukon knew little of the use of guns except for hunting. They would never consider the cowboy techniques of the "quick draw artists," who would shoot a man on sight and ask questions later. Canadians were appalled by the wanton thievery and the roaming cut-throats they encountered at Skagway and Wrangell.

The provincial government in Victoria and the federal government in Ottawa worked together to bring some sense of order to the immediate chaos. One of the first laws they agreed on was that no person would be allowed to enter the north without adequate provisions. The starvation endured earlier at Dawson was a lesson no one wished repeated. While governments dealt with laws and customs, Kate began her own plans and organization. Directed by an advertisement in the Vancouver *Daily Colonist*, Kate picked up a government brochure at the post office. This brochure listed the supplies required by law for one person to survive one year in the Canadian north. To enforce compliance, the brochure told its readers, officers of the North West Mounted Police stationed at border points would turn back anyone who did not have the specified provisions. At first, Kate thought the quantities seemed immense: eight 50-pound sacks of flour, 150 pounds of bacon, 150 pounds of split peas, 100 pounds of beans, 75 pounds of canned fruit, 100 pounds of granulated sugar, eight pounds of baking powder, four dozen one-pound cans of condensed milk. Next on the list came the work items: one pick, an extra handle, a drift pick, one shovel, one gold pan, one axe, a sleeping bag, a fur coat, matches and a Bible. The list went on and on: one knife, one fork, one pie plate . . . Kate was sure that one outfit would have completely filled the shelves of her father's store in Johnville.

Purchasing these supplies would take a large part of Kate's hard-earned money, which she wanted to spend wisely. Having assessed the Vancouver outfitters, Kate headed for the Hudson Bay Company and asked for the manager. No doubt she would pay extra for her goods, but to take a chance with some of the swindlers advertising rock-bottom prices did not seem to be worth the risk. She wanted the assurance that every dollar spent was wisely invested. Besides, everyone knew that the initials H.B.C. stood for "Here Before Christ." The institution that had planted its standard on the Pacific North generations before should have expert knowledge about the best equipment for a woman heading into the interior. Gathering her propriety around her, Kate followed Robert Lockyer, the Hudson Bay Company manager, to the elevator. This convenience had the effect of a time machine; the doors closed on the fashionable main floor and, a few seconds later, opened on "Siberia."

To serve the immense gold rush trade, the Hudson Bay Company had hastily renovated the top storey of its building to accommodate the supplies needed for northern expeditions. The floor was piled high with every conceivable piece of equipment. Racks were crowded with parkas, long coats, short coats, fur coats and mackinaws. Tents were piled in tiers and boxes spilled their contents at random. Lockyer stepped expertly around the piles as he summoned a clerk to bring a chair for his customer.

"Now, Mrs. Ryan, first we must determine size. Are the clothes for your husband?"

With an Irish twinkle in her eyes, Kate smoothed the folds of her dress with her large hands and looked directly at the manager.

"Oh, no, sir, you are confused. It is Miss Ryan, Kate if you will, and the boots and the coat must fit me. It is I who is going to the Yukon."

For a moment, Lockyer seemed to have a problem with his throat, though he quickly regained his composure. But when Kate began to laugh, he joined her heartily. He put away his manager's formal manner, and to Kate's delight, spent the next two hours helping her choose every item necessary for her adventure. Mr. Lockyer — Robert by now — had a lot of experience in outfitting travellers to the gold fields. He suggested that sturdy work boots would prove more useful than fashionable ladies' boots, and a mackinaw would be easier to get around in than a heavy fur coat. Besides the fact that the fur coat cost twice as much, he confided, the Company had received a large order of fur coats for the North West Mounted Police, but the commander had ordered the coats shortened. They were so heavy the men could not carry them, let alone wade through snow in them. Another item that took careful consideration was a rifle. Robert repeated to the reluctant Kate the advice of William Ogilvie, whose word was considered gospel: "When you want a weapon you want it bad, suppose you were to come upon a bear and his time had come, what a fix you would be in if you couldn't fulfil the decree." The yarn convinced even the tenderfoot Kate that she must have a rifle, and finally she settled on a Winchester. It weighed less than the Marlin, and Kate decided that with a little practice she would feel comfortable with it. The clerks in "Siberia" moved goods from one pile to another at a frenzied pace until at last Kate's outfit completely surrounded her. With her own list checked off, she asked Robert if she had forgotten anything. He made his way back through the maze and returned carrying a small black travelling bag decorated with a bright brass locking clasp. He opened it and showed her the several compartments and the small secret pocket in the false bottom. The bag exuded the rich, sweet scent of new leather. Kate hesitated as she stroked the smooth finish.

"It is indeed a beautiful bag, but I'm afraid it would just be too expensive," she said, sighing.

"Miss Ryan, I mean Kate, please accept this from our company," Lockyer responded. "Any lady with the courage to head out to the Yukon on her own deserves the support of the Hudson Bay Company. My only request is that, if there is anything I can send to you, or any service we can offer, please write and I will comply immediately."

Kate graciously accepted the gift, and with a firm promise to keep Robert Lockyer informed about her travels, left the Hudson Bay store with her spirits soaring. Her dream was becoming a reality.

With her provision problem solved, Kate now considered transportation. At the steamship office, after much haggling with the overworked and anxious ticket agent, she booked her passage from Vancouver on February 28, 1898, on the steamer *Tees*. Then she had to make her most difficult decision: selecting a method of travel in the north. According to all the rumours and stories that were circulating, she had two choices, dogs or horses. Ordinarily, horses would be her first choice, but she had heard they were next to impossible to obtain. Nevertheless, she made her way to the Vancouver stockyards. The lessons of childhood came back to Kate as she inspected the poor horses in the sale pens. It took her only a few minutes to realize the sorry state of horse flesh in southern British Columbia. Among these poor creatures old Queenie would have looked like a champion. A fellow New Brunswicker described in his daily journal the six horses he was forced to purchase, and his assessment later appeared in a newspaper. "They are ambulating bone-yards, the infirm and decrepit, those afflicted with spavin and spring halt, and many with ribs like the sides of whiskey casks and hips to hang hats on. With their drooping heads and listless tails, they are indeed pictures of misfortune."

Kate tried bartering with the horse traders, but they had little time for a woman and didn't even wait to see if she had any money. They had animals that they could get any price for, and they considered only the highest bidder. For $30, the best Kate could hope for would be an old packer; a $25 horse was worthless. She could not invest her remaining savings on any of those sad equine specimens, and so she decided to look for a reasonably priced team of good dogs. Just a week earlier, the *Daily Colonist* had reported that Captain David Barnett had invested $1,700 in one team of malmutes. With this unbelievable price ringing in her head, Kate began her search for a less expensive team. After more than a week of searching, she gave a man a $100 down payment from her dwindling savings and agreed to pay the remainder when he delivered her new team of five grey huskies and a cedar sled to the *Tees.*

Now Kate began to tidy up her last business affairs and put together her own personal belongings. In the small notebook in which she kept her journal, she had listed her supplies and costs. As a final check, she eliminated anything that she felt was not absolutely necessary and, to contradict herself, added a few items that she had forgotten. Then she packed her most precious possessions into the small black bag that Robert had given her. Meticulously she folded one good dress, a few other pieces of clothing, four yards of sturdy cotton, sewing supplies, her rosary and her missal. Next she added her medical supplies, bandages

Kate with dog-sled team. (KMK)

and the medicine bottles wrapped individually and placed in a protective box. In the secret compartment she laid the cameo necklace that Simon had given to her. She had never removed it from its burgundy velvet case, and she put her memories away with it in the bottom of the leather bag. There she also placed the remainder of her savings, including a five dollar gold piece that Moses and Lou Brennan had given to her. Moses said it was his investment. He regretted that he couldn't join the gold rush himself, but he knew that whatever business Kate invested in would succeed. The last package was a small handful of Johnville soil that her mother had made her take along when she left home years before. Kate had not yet found a permanent home for the soil or for herself; perhaps she would find that special place in the Yukon. With a sense of pride and accomplishment, she snapped the brass clasp shut. Her packing was finished; she was ready.

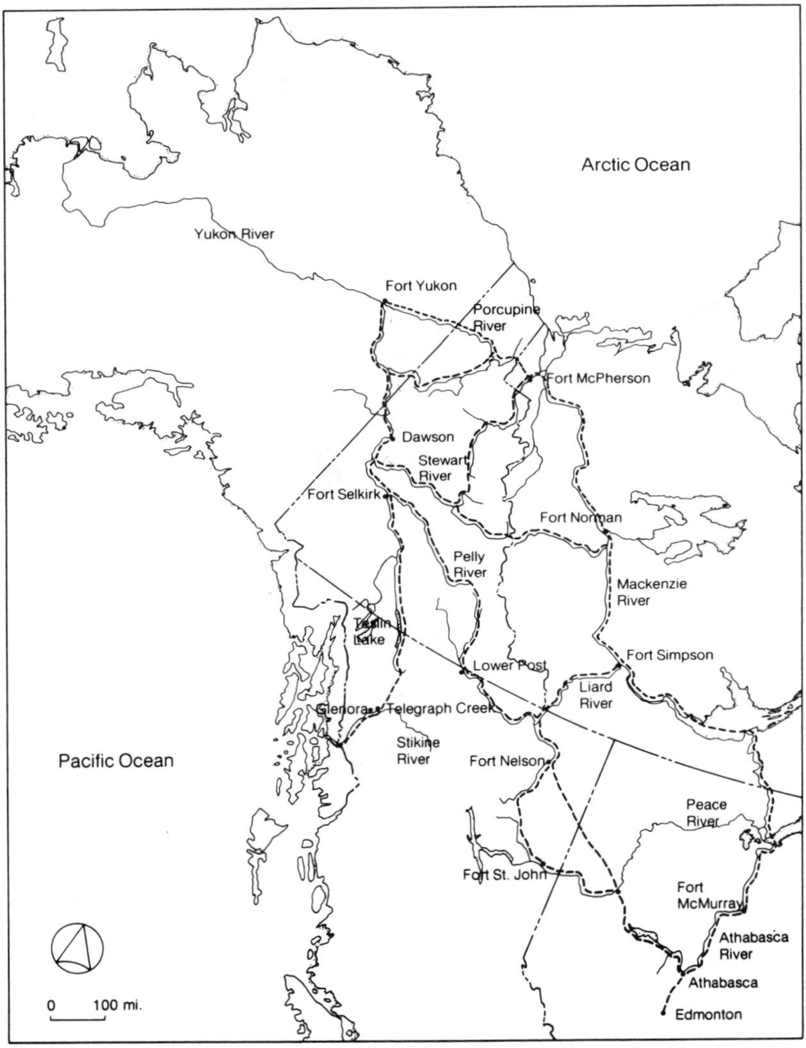

The Stikine Route and main Edmonton routes to the Klondike.

(map by S. Epps)

The Stikine Route

The excitement aboard the Canadian Navigation steamer *Tees* was electric. When the whistles blared "all ashore," Moses and Lou Brennan bid Kate a hasty farewell. They waved from the dock, and Kate returned their waves as the laughter and shouts from shore and the noise from the ship drowned out their last good-byes. The deck hands pulled in the hawsers and the steamer slipped its moorings, edging its way out of the Vancouver harbour. The passenger list of the *Tees* read like a who's who of men and women from all over the globe, all caught up in the frenzy of the Klondike Gold Rush. The passengers represented every social class and profession imaginable, but among the lawyers, doctors and fortune hunters there were a few authentic, experienced prospectors. They were the only ones with even the slightest idea of the hardships that lay ahead.

Kate took a while to find her sea legs. Uncomfortable on the water, she would have chosen any other mode of travel if any had existed, but she determined to make the best of the journey. On the first day out of port, the *Tees* followed the sheltered passage up the Strait of Georgia until, near nightfall, it reached open water. The Pacific Ocean greeted the *Tees* with a gale force wind and pounding rain. Those who had gathered in the main lounge for the first evening social retreated to their cramped berths to weather the storm. Most of the night the steamer was rocked and buffeted by the howling winds. Not until the early hours of the morning did the storm subside. Finally Kate fell into a fitful sleep, only to be plagued by nightmares of shipwrecks. The early morning sounds of the shipboard activities awakened her, and she felt grateful to have survived the storms of the night, both real and imaginary.

After breakfast, the passengers continued to promenade the deck in spite of the cutting wind that persisted most of the day. On the lee side, men huddled in small groups smoking their pipes and gossiping. Other small groups played cards between the dunnage bales, out of the wind. When Kate finally regained her courage, she joined the strollers on deck to take in the spectacular scenery. Deep fjords and inlets broke the rough coast. The mountains came to the very water's edge, spilling cascades of crystal snow water into the channel. Breathing deeply of the cold sharp air, Kate began to relax and enjoy her voyage.

The *Tees* was a new vessel, outfitted with the most modern materials and equipment. Beauty and expert workmanship characterized the passenger accommodations. The ornamental mouldings were painted white and accented with gold. The walls and bar were finished in the finest red mahogany enriched with brass railings. Expensive furniture and hangings added to the luxury of the vessel. The only precaution the crew had taken to protect the steamer from the overflow of animals and passengers was to cover the carpets and hardwood floors with grey canvas.

The cargo hold was filled beyond capacity. Cattle, horses and bales of freight overflowed the hold and spilled out onto the lower decks. Even the sleeping cabins and passageways were piled with suitcases and boxes of every shape and size, so that only narrow lanes allowed the passengers to navigate the obstacle course to their berths. On the upper deck, every corner had been converted into extra sleeping accommodations. Four berths had been arranged on the platform above the broad companionway that led to the dining cabin. This exposed the second class passengers who slept there to public view at every meal. Undaunted, they took the opportunity to lie in their berths chatting with those waiting in line to eat. And meal times were the high points of the day. Diners congregated early, sitting in ranks on the companionway waiting for the gong to sound. At its first tone, they rushed to the tables and devoured the food as if it were the last they would ever see. Then they returned to the deck to indulge in a cigar and wait for the ritual to be repeated.

Kate soon discovered that the *Tees* was a virtual Noah's Ark, overflowing with animals of all descriptions. Besides the expected contingent of dogs, there was an assortment of chickens, ducks and goats collected in strange-looking crates. At one end of the deck, a not-very-contented cow made her presence known both vocally and by the slippery flapjacks that kept getting in the way of the promenading ladies. The animals demanded as much attention as the human cargo, keeping two men busy carrying food to them and then shovelling the droppings overboard — "the natural cycle of Mother Nature," observed a veteran lounging on the piled freight. All day the calliope of yelping, barking and bawling continued, and on into the night. If the din subsided for a few minutes, some discontented malamute would yelp his sadness to the mountains, and the chorus would begin again, accompanied by curses and flying objects.

On the second evening out of port, the passengers once again gathered in the lounge, successful this time in organizing a rousing singsong. Many had brought along their own musical instruments, and soon the strains of songs and melodies floated over the water. Popular songs such as "There'll Be A Hot Time In The Old Town Tonight" and "Where Is My Wandering Boy Tonight?" seemed appropriate for the travellers. As her passengers made merry, the *Tees* plunged onward past the Queen Charlotte Islands into the Dixon Entrance.

The steamer met other ships on their return voyages from the north, and as they passed one another those who had been to the Klondike waved energetically to the passengers of the *Tees*, trying frantically to signal their own disappointment and to caution others to return home. But their pleas and shouts of advice were ignored as the *Tees* and her passengers continued northward toward their destiny. As the faint light of dawn broke through the grey morning on the fourth day of the voyage, the *Tees* edged carefully through the ice-speckled waters of Clarence Strait.

From the old-timers returning to the Klondike, Kate learned that the previous summer the port of Wrangell had been nothing more than a woodstop for steamers plying their trade between Alaskan ports and Seattle. The "town" had consisted of five wooden structures, a few tents and a saloon. Originally an Indian village, Wrangell had sprung to commercial life during the Cassiar gold rush in the early 1870s, and slowly the Siwash culture had merged with the white man's confusion. By the time Kate and her fellow passengers saw the town, its second economic boom had brought it to total confusion and chaos.

The captain of the *Tees* manoeuvred his steamer up to the

dilapidated dock. But the tide was out and the spindly wharf piles stilted out of the water, and so the captain had to lie offshore until the tide could bring the steamer close enough to the dock to unload. With the cold wind blowing snow and icy rain, and a grey fog hanging over most of the lowland, the town presented a desolate sight for the enthusiastic passengers. When Kate was finally able to disembark, the solid ground felt so welcome under her feet that she silently vowed henceforth to leave water travel to others.

The land did not offer much comfort because the early spring rains had turned the beach area into a mire of slush, mud and manure. The wharfs and every piece of ground was crowded with boxes, crates, suitcases and bales. The beach was littered with stoves, lumber, oil drums, dog sleds and tents. In every open space, men, horses, dogs, mules, cows, oxen and even goats roamed at will, compounding the confusion and deepening the mire. Men appeared to take command, shouting orders to move stores and supplies to make room for more, but as soon as they disappeared others trying equally hard to sort out the mess contradicted their orders. As the crew of the *Tees* tried desperately to unload freight, the booms and hoists swinging between ship and shore broke regularly, spilling goods and parcels over the wharf.

As she watched the scene, Kate realized that she was about to assert her complete independence. If she wanted to have her own outfit intact, she would have to supervise the unloading herself. Singling out a crew member with whom she had been friendly during the voyage, she managed to get the dogs unloaded. Hastily she led them to an open area away from the beach. Relieved to be out of captivity, the dogs lunged for freedom, but, taking full control of them as of her own life, she led them to a spot behind a windbreak. Tying them to some scrub cedars, she established her cache. She rummaged through her own bags to retrieve her Hudson Bay travelling clothes. At once she donned the heavy boots and rough mackinaw, thanking Robert Lockyer *in absentia* for his wisdom. Properly dressed, she returned to the steamer for the remainder of her outfit.

It took Kate the best part of the day to get her possessions unloaded and deposited at her depot. As she worked, she listened to the conversations around her, trying to calculate where she was and what the next move would be. Part of the confusion was caused by the fact that Wrangell was on an island. The only way to move any further was to secure another passage on one of the small steamers transporting goods across to Cottonwood Island, from which she could continue on the ice to the mainland. Once she reached the mainland, she had thirty more miles to trek to the Canadian boundary and the start of the All Canadian Route.

Kate soon discovered that the steamers carrying goods to Cottonwood Island could navigate the channel only at high tide and were constantly running aground on the sand bars in the inlet. Then she found out about the complicated business practices of the Wrangell shipping companies and customs brokers. The companies that had built the flimsy wharfs levied a charge of $2 per ton on all freight landing on their docks and an extra 25¢ on each piece of baggage over the prescribed size. Facing the oversized foreman, Kate had to pay up without discussion, only to face the customs broker, who charged $5 to bond each outfit and mark it with an official American seal; no boxes could be opened until they reached Canadian territory. Then she had to deal with the inspector, the American government representative in charge of everything, and at least two junior functionaries in charge of anything that the others forgot to mention. All charged for their mandatory services. The last unpleasant official informed her that another agent at the Canadian boundary would ensure that all was done correctly and that he, too, would receive his just fee.

It was late in the day when Kate finally had a fire going and a real opportunity to survey her new surroundings. Wrangell was a strange mixture of new wooden structures which elbowed out the more indigenous-looking homes of the native Siwash. The moss-covered roofs and decaying walls showed that the native houses had stood in that place for more than fifty years. Totem poles guarded them, their carvings of beast, bird, fish and ancient gods representing the Siwash heraldry. The ferocious faces of the totems seemed to glare at the passing crowds of white trespassers.

The main street of Wrangell tried to follow the shore, but

walking along it proved to be a challenge because of mud holes, ruts and debris. Makeshift restaurants, saloons, dance halls, general merchants, money lenders and outfitting companies lined both sides of the thoroughfare, all thriving. Behind the main street, a labyrinth of footpaths led to more stores and dwelling places. In the distance, on the east point that appeared to be guarding the inner harbour, Kate could see a sawmill. It was in full operation, converting huge spruce and fir logs into lumber rumoured to be so green that, when a floor made of them dried, a man could disappear through the cracks and never be seen again. Still, lumber was in such great demand that unplaned boards sold for $22 per thousand feet.

Of the thousands of would-be gold seekers who landed in this miserable village, many stayed only until they got sick of the whole idea and returned south in disgust. But at least one of the more adventurous, who, like Kate, was also much more optimistic, went so far as to create a vision of Wrangell in poetry. Henry Woodside, a writer and surveyor as well as a daring adventurer, wrote:

> Behind the Indian's bark canoes
> The steamer rocks and waves
> And city lots are staked for sale
> Above old Indian graves.

Like Henry, Kate was far from discouraged. She set out to see just what this notorious town of Wrangell was all about. The men and the few women she saw and spoke to were a strange lot from all corners of the world. A few of the men warned her to be careful, because, they claimed, they had been robbed, but a more seasoned pioneer told her that anyone who minded their own business and stayed away from the gambling places and saloons would be safe enough. Taking his advice to heart, she made her way to the steamer office to purchase a ticket for Cottonwood Island, but the ticket agent gave only vague answers about time of departure, assuring her only that someone would fetch her when they could load her gear. When she returned to her campsite, she expected to get word to move on in a few hours, and so she did not set up her tent. Instead, she spent the time close to her cache, feeding her dogs and running them to the river for exercise to keep them quiet and under control. She realized by watching her neighbours that she must keep her dogs tethered, for roaming animals caused untold damage and nuisance for their owners and the other unwilling shore-dwellers.

The hours of waiting turned into days. On the second day, Kate watched a troop of North West Mounted Police set up their camp a few hundred yards away from her own. She was impressed with the control and discipline exercised by their commander, who seemed to have complete authority over the men going about their duties with cheerful order. This spectacle contrasted so sharply with everything else in Wrangell that some of the shore inhabitants actually welcomed them and offered their help. Even though they were still in American territory, Kate felt much safer with the Mounties camped beside her.

After her second night in the open, wrapped in a sleeping bag and catching only a few hours of sleep, Kate began to worry that she would never cross to the mainland if she did not take action. She presented herself at the police bivouac, where a clean-shaven young constable eagerly introduced himself.

"Morning, Ma'am, name is George Chalmers. Would you have a cup of coffee?" Without waiting for a reply he passed Kate a cup of the strongest brew she had ever tasted. His barrage of conversation gave Kate a complete outline of the detachment and the news of the day. The commanding officer, Inspector Phillip Primrose, was away trying to secure accommodations on the ferry for his men. This was the information that Kate needed, so she decided to wait for Inspector Primrose's return. Chalmers then took Kate into his confidence.

"Ma'am, I am in a bad fix. The Inspector fired the cook the first thing this morning for spending the night in a Wrangell saloon and, being the junior of the detachment, the job of cook fell on me, and Ma'am, I don't know the first thing about cooking, let alone cooking for a crew of men. When I saw you walking across the shore I just knew you were sent from heaven."

Judging by the coffee, Kate believed Chalmers when he said he knew very little about cooking, but she laughed at his flattery.

"Well, I'll make a deal with you," she offered. "You promise to put away your compliments and stop trying to make an angel out of me, and I'll help you get started. It doesn't look as if I'm going anywhere for a while anyway."

With the young constable following close on her heels, they set about building a fire in the camp stove leaning precariously in the wind. Between them, they had biscuits made and pork frying when Inspector Primrose returned to camp. If he was surprised to see a woman at his campsite, he did not let on. He offered Kate a polite greeting and kept the men busy until the meal was ready. When Chalmers clanged the camp bell, the ravenous men fell upon the food, delighting Kate with their comments about Chalmers's ability to cook so well with so little experience. As they cleaned up afterwards, each man in turn gave Kate his heartfelt thanks for such a great feed. Obviously they had not eaten so well for a long time. Late that evening, when the chores were done and the men were sitting around the camp fire, Primrose invited Kate into his tent.

Phillip Carteret Hill Primrose, a handsome man of thirty-four, was already a seasoned veteran of the North West Mounted Police. He had joined immediately after his graduation from Royal Military College in 1885 and had been posted first at Regina and then at Fort Saskatchewan and Fort McLeod. His strength of character and his reputation made him one of Clifford Sifton's first choices for the difficult work that had to be done in the Yukon. The police force was Primrose's life, and he ruled his men by the strict code of his own military training. The North West Mounted Police force now under his command was to prove one of his most important northern assignments. Clifford Sifton himself had ordered him to secure the Canadian boundary between British Columbia and the Alaskan Panhandle, and Primrose and his detachment had complete jurisdiction over the stampeders coming and going along the proposed All Canadian Route through the Stikine territory. Under his command, he had several experienced leaders, including Sergeant Major Malcolm McDonell and the company medical officer, Dr. Fraser. Once they established their post at the Canadian-American border, Customs Officer John Turner would take charge of inspecting incoming cargo and travellers to make sure each person had all the provisions judged necessary to survive in the north. Turner would also have to ensure that they carried no illegal gambling devices, liquor or offensive weapons.

The North West Mounted Police detachment had another job to do in the Stikine territory besides acting as customs inspectors and policing the trails. On January 26, 1898, the Canadian Government had signed a contract with William McKenzie and Donald Mann, who agreed to build a wagon road that would link the Stikine River steamer route with a proposed narrow-gauge railway to be built from the head of navigation on the Stikine River to Teslin Lake. To complete the All Canadian Route, the government planned to connect the northern end of the rail line with another fleet of steamboats to be built on Teslin Lake. This contract became one of the most celebrated in the history of Canadian politics. When its terms became known, the House of Commons cried scandal and patronage, because, in return for their labours, McKenzie and Mann were to receive a land grant of 25,000 acres for each mile of railway they constructed, along with a huge but undisclosed sum of money. Sifton assured parliament that this transportation system would open the Klondike gold fields to the benefit of Canadians, and that Canadian interests were well protected by the North West Mounted Police. This general protection of Canadian interests was one of the tasks taking Phillip Primrose and his band into the interior.

But the affairs of government were of little interest to Kate, stranded as she was in American territory and subject to the heavy tariffs and fees the officials unjustly imposed on travellers. The Americans took particular delight in "skinning" their Canadian neighbours, convinced that a treaty would soon decree that the Alaskan panhandle belonged to them. Primrose was brusque and to the point. The ferry operators were clearly abusing their authority and grafting every cent they could from everyone stranded in Wrangell. Having watched their methods that afternoon, Primrose saw that crews were putting the steamers on the sand bars deliberately to play havoc with the passengers and delay travel. Because the ferries had gambling games and well-stocked bars aboard, they were in no hurry to lose their passengers. If Kate intended to go on to Canadian territory, she would have to pay extra for her passage. Primrose himself had succumbed that day and reluctantly made a deal with the wharf thieves. Now he had to wait for results. Kate had little cash left. Knowing she would face more duties at the Canadian boundary, she balked at paying a second fare. After a few moments' thought, she offered Primrose her own proposition. If he would allow her to accompany his contingent to the Canadian boundary, she would gladly offer her services as a cook. Primrose had to admit that the evening meal was the first good food he had tasted in a long time, and he did not look forward to any more of Chalmers's food or coffee. With a grin he agreed to the offer and attached the name Ryan, K. to his detachment's passenger list.

A third day passed without any progress. As the men went about their camp duties, Kate decided to go into Wrangell for yeast and a few other supplies before they went on the trail. At Chalmers's suggestion she went into the "den of thieves" to seek out the notorious baker of Wrangell, Alex Burghardt. Her nose led her to his tent. She had heard that Burghardt was as proficient at cards and dice as he was at baking, but, dressed in his stained, flour-covered apron, he greeted Kate graciously. Soon he had introduced her to cooking bread and biscuits Yukon style, with sourdough. During the opening of the north, even the most basic supplies were at times impossible to obtain. Cooks would keep a small portion of the bread dough from one raising until the next. This unused dough sat in a warm crock, where it fermented and became sour. When this starter was added to fresh flour and water, its fermentation would act as yeast, and it gave the resulting bread and biscuits a special flavour and texture. Thus the name "sourdough" stuck to the early travellers into the north country. Thanking baker Burghardt for her first northern cooking lesson, Kate returned to camp with her "sourdough starter" in a lard kettle. She tried her first batch of sourdough biscuits on the men for supper and was delighted by their hearty approval.

The police force and Kate maintained their watch on the beach. After four days, they finally received word to pack up for the first ferry at daylight. When the *Louise* deposited Kate on the west shore of Cottonwood Island, she found that her dogs, supplies and tent were all in a complete tangle, the same sight that had greeted her eyes in Wrangell. The steamer crews had little regard for personal possessions and threw supplies at will along the shore line. The island itself was covered with three feet of hard-packed snow that gave way under the weight of the heavy boxes and animals that struggled to free themselves of their burdens. Luckily, Primrose arrived. He ordered some men to set up camp and sent two constables to collect the frightened animals. The rest of the group made a brave attempt to sort out supplies and determine the damage suffered under the hands of the crew of the steamer. When her own supplies were untangled, Kate considered herself lucky, as all her goods were accounted for, and except for a few broken boxes, everything seemed to be in order. The Indian guide Inspector Primrose had acquired in Wrangell had already proved his usefulness by shooting a moose. The aroma of moosemeat frying over the campfire soon wafted over the trees, putting everyone back in good spirits. The night surrounded them, and a huge bonfire lit the sky. The sweet melody of a harmonica mingled with the crackling of the fire.

But on the trail nothing was ever constant. After they had all bedded down, the temperature suddenly dropped, and Kate huddled with the others as close as possible to the fire. At first light, the men rose quickly and moved about, trying to warm their aching bodies. Breakfast consisted of extra strong coffee and hunks of frozen bread smothered with molasses. The grey light of morning filtered through the trees as the men prepared to break camp and start their first day up the frozen Stikine River on the first leg of the All Canadian Route to the Yukon gold fields. Four junior constables led the first group up the trail with five teams of horses and three dog sleds. They loaded the animals lightly because they wanted to test the snow pack on the trail ahead. The guide warned Primrose that the trail was going to be rough and the horses would not make it over the crust with heavy loads. Kate stayed with the main group that would start a little behind the leaders. Two men would remain on Cottonwood Island with the relief animals and the additional supplies until the trail was prepared for them. Previous explorers claimed that the Stikine River was the most treacherous waterway in the world. Now it lay impotent, frozen beneath their feet, but they had to reach their first destination before the weather changed and turned their road into a turbulent river again.

The frozen Stikine River snaked its way through a deep canyon for the first fifty miles upstream. In the distance, the mountain peak called Kate's Needle stabbed 10,000 feet into the air. On the north side of the rocky wall rose the Choquette Glacier. Alexander Choquette had been the first white man to prospect the Stikine River. He found gold, and in 1862 his discovery caused a gold rush that brought 800 men up the Stikine. Only half of them made it to the gold fields; the elements and the river overpowered the rest. Twelve years later, the discovery of gold in the Cassiar district caused a second gold rush in 1874. Now, in 1898, men lusting for gold once again began to pour into the Stikine seeking a route that would lead them to the Klondike and the greatest gold discovery the world had ever known.

Primrose and his men had not yet been struck by gold fever, but they were passionate about protecting their country and the responsibility of the job that now confronted them. Having just witnessed a little of the effect of the gold rush in Wrangell, they began to imagine its larger consequences. First, they had to establish a post and base camp at the Canadian boundary. As they began their journey toward that goal, they found the trail in pretty good condition for the first few miles. By mid-morning, however, they began to run into slush and water at intervals. It did not improve, and as the day wore on, travelling became a horrible ordeal for both men and animals. A thin layer of hard-packed snow overlay an accumulation of snow and ice up to ten feet thick. When a loaded pack horse broke through the crust it could literally drown in the snow if the men did not haul it out in time. Holes made this way had to be repaired immediately, so that the rest of the party could pass over the same trail. On Sunday night, Kate and the North West Mounted Police detachment made camp on the opposite side of the river just below the site known as Dewdney Camp. The scouts reported that horses could not possibly proceed any further along the trail, so they set up a secondary camp, and Primrose dispatched men to return to Cottonwood Island to bring up the remainder of the men and supplies.

Light snow fell as the team set off. It continued to snow or rain most of the time during the next few days, and every morn-

The North West Mounted Police post known as the Dewdney Camp, spring, 1898. This post marked the boundary line for the beginning of the All Canadian Route. (HJW/NAC)

ing two inches of water covered the river ice. The men at the camp moved the supplies and animals across the river to the Dewdney site. On March 9, Primrose selected a building site on high ground, as close as his best guess could make it to the Canadian-American boundary line. Later, a survey confirmed that the spot he chose was 800 yards inside Canada. During the rest of that day, the men repaired the trail, arranged the stores and settled down to wait for the remainder of their party. Once they had returned with the rest of the supplies, the whole detachment began to build the outpost and the customs building, firmly planting Canadian authority on the Stikine River and in the Province of British Columbia. A sense of permanence and relief came over the men at the Dewdney site. They were back on Canadian soil, and with Inspector Primrose in charge they could take over their responsibility for law and order. An intangible feeling of security and well-being surrounded the camp.

Back on Canadian soil, Kate, preparing to begin her own trek up the still-frozen river, got her gear ready to leave at first light and retired early. Suddenly, in the very early hours of the morning, the temperature rose and a warm chinook wind blew down the valley, changing the mild snow to torrential rain. Kate woke with a start, lying in a torrent of rushing water. She knew her most dreaded fear had come true — the river had melted. But as she gained her senses and rushed outside, she realized that a flood of water cascading down the sides of the canyon walls had created a turbulent stream through the camp. Kate and the men knew there would be no more sleep that night and huddled around the campfire until dawn trying to dry out their clothes and sleeping bags.

Despite the horrible winter conditions, large numbers of men and animals already dotted the trail. The Inspector and his men were dumbfounded by the numbers who had struggled up the unusual roadway to the north ahead of them. In his sessional report to headquarters, Primrose described what he and his men had seen:

> During this time the trail all along until the ice became unsafe, was a string of struggling, tugging, pulling humanity. Cheerful withal, which is to be wondered at, when you consider endless numbers of these people had to relay three times; so if they had to get through the 150 miles to Glenora you can easily see the amount of travel which they would have to do.

Heading out, Kate was continually amazed to meet groups of men along the trail. They blended with the environment as if they were intended to be there, and strangest of all, a carnival atmosphere lay over the frozen river trail.

The Town that was Built in a Day

History records that in the months of February and March, 1898, one thousand voyagers inched their way along the icy trail between Wrangell, Alaska and Glenora, British Columbia. Inspector Primrose described in his reports the cheerful and optimistic atmosphere in the Stikine country during the spring of '98, as the gold seekers began their adventure into the wilderness. The fortune ahead seemed assured, and the physical inconveniences were a small price to pay for the final victory. Men without pack animals had to move their supplies on their own backs. They carried one load over a few hundred yards of the trail and then returned for another load, continuing this procedure until they had moved their stores up the river. Every hundred yards was an accomplishment, each mile a celebration. Only those with experience in the wilderness and those with tremendous physical strength made it through to the outpost at Glenora.

The first day after Kate left the Dewdney camp, the weather was cold and clear, and the cloud cover kept the sun from melting the trail. By evening she guessed she had covered about eight miles, a significant distance. Once she had her campfire blazing securely, she fed her dogs and then returned to the fire to consider her own hunger pains. Her kettle slung over the fire soon boiled, and into it she dropped some chunks of frozen meat and two of her precious potatoes, also frozen. Intent on her supper, she did not hear a visitor approach. She turned suddenly at the sound of a voice behind her asking if she might have enough in the pot for a hungry visitor. Kate did not rise but continued to stir the boiling kettle while she assessed her uninvited guest. Judging by his silhouette in the dusk, her visitor was a tall, thin man who seemed to be travelling light. He shouldered a heavy knapsack and carried a canvas bag, but he had no other gear. This seemed strange to Kate, considering the burdens most on the trail had to carry, but his pleasant, cheerful voice reassured her. He began to talk and ask questions at the same time, without waiting for answers. This conversational style suited Kate just fine.

"How do you do?" he asked. "Mind if I stop for a spell? Saw your fire a way back and thought there would be no need for both of us to build a fire. The name is Pringle, John Pringle. And who might you be, sir?"

Kate beckoned Pringle to join her at the fire, and as he chaffed his hands he continued his monologue.

"No clouds in the sky, tomorrow should be another good day for travelling. I didn't catch your name, sir."

Kate rose and faced Pringle, offering her hand with a grin.

"My word, you are a woman! I do beg your pardon, Madam, I never expected to meet a woman here in the wilderness."

Kate poured him a cup of coffee from her steaming pot and asked him if he was afraid of a woman. Embarrassed, he accepted the coffee as he composed himself and began to laugh at his own ramblings. But after apologizing, he compounded the insult by inquiring if Kate's husband was about.

"No husband, sir, I am here on my own," Kate replied curtly. "Have the bit of stew left in the pot," she added, to avoid any continuation of the subject. She did not want to pursue the questions she knew he had on the tip of his tongue. Taking the hint, Pringle pulled a log forward and graciously accepted one of Kate's two precious potatoes. Kate found John Pringle's chattering a relief. She was tired of answering questions about being in the wilderness by herself. She was content — why wasn't everyone else? A secretive person, she wanted to listen and learn and keep her business to herself. The reactions caused by her solitude annoyed her, and she hated having to defend her presence every time she turned around. But Pringle obligingly nattered on about his own life and travels, and before they finished their supper Kate knew most of his life story. Reverend John Pringle, a native of Prince Edward Island, was a Presbyterian minister, a devout Christian with fire and passion in his heart. His church had sent him to the new frontier as a missionary to the adventurers in the northern wilderness. His superiors envisioned the need for a man of good character to lend a hand to his fellows in the north, and when they selected John Pringle they chose the most able man in all of Canada for the job. Pringle would himself become a legend in his own time. An outspoken man, he was determined to save souls whether they wished to be saved or not. He was honest, truthful to a fault, totally and completely opposed to gambling and liquor and an unquestioning Laurier man. In spite of his religion and his overwhelming manner, Kate decided that she liked the Reverend Mr. Pringle.

Kate had a habit of assessing people immediately. When she was a young girl, her mother Anne teased her about her sixth sense and told her she had "the gift," whatever that meant. Whether she had "the gift" or just strong instincts, she was seldom wrong about people. John Pringle was also intuitive. It was his business to assess people, and he realized immediately that here was a competent woman without fear of the elements. He knew that anyone with those qualities must have a great faith in God; Kate must be a good woman, even if she was a Catholic. Not only that, but during the conversation they discovered their mutual Maritime roots and the places and friends they both knew. As the flames turned to embers, Pringle threw a heavy log on the fire and spread his bedroll for another night under the stars. In the distance, other campfires shone their welcome beacons, and the night sounds of the north mingled with the barking of the coyotes in the distance.

Deep in the interior, eighty miles upriver, the settlement of Glenora also lay quietly content. Isolated from the world outside, the community slept and awaited spring. The town consisted of three merchants, two packing outfits, a few settlers and the occasional Indian. None of these had any inkling that their quiet world was about to be invaded. James Callbreath was the owner of the trading post and a leader of the community. He had come to the Stikine territory during the Cassiar gold rush in 1874. He did not find the gold he sought, but he fell in love with the wild country and decided to make Glenora his home, finally convincing himself that he was content with the quieter life and would never again go off in search of the illusive wealth. Word of the Yukon gold strike had long since reached Glenora, and Jim had been the government surveyor who had charted the Stikine country for Sifton's All Canadian Route. Even so, he remained sceptical of the rumours and wild stories. He had heard it all before. Having already lived to witness two other gold strikes, he believed he would watch this one come and go with little effect on his way of life.

With the survey crew, Jim had spent the preceding summer in the interior traversing every possible route to Teslin Lake. Then he had travelled to Victoria to present his findings in person to Sifton and his colleagues. He had been emphatic in his recommendations: "It would be inconceivable to build a railway through the swamp above Telegraph Creek to get to Teslin Lake. The practical solution would be a wagon road between Telegraph Creek and Teslin Lake." But it was clear to Jim that the government officials had already made up their minds. They were not interested in his logic and knowledge of the interior; instead, they were determined to go ahead with their contract with McKenzie & Mann for the construction of this railway, no matter how impractical. As the months went by, Jim held out hope that, if the proposed route ever did get to Glenora, they would get their much needed road before the whole episode was over. If they could at least accomplish that much, the railway foolishness would be worth something. Now, with the warm days of March upon them, the residents of Glenora waited to see what spring would bring. Early in the month, a few weary travellers began to trickle into town. All had great dreams and hopes for the future, and all had promises from various government officials that a railroad would be built at the first signs of spring breakup. Everyone would be in the Yukon by late summer.

Among the first few adventurers to make it through to Glenora on the frozen Stikine were Kate Ryan and the Reverend John Pringle. Jim had bragged that he had seen everything in previous gold rushes, but the appearance of a woman on her own confounded even him. Her very presence, her independent manner and her ability to cope in the wilderness suited the rough packer's code of ethics. As far as Jim and his associates were concerned, "any woman who could make it up the Stikine River on the ice should be treated as an equal with any packer in the territory."

The stampeders brought precious news to Glenora, including

newspapers reporting on the progress of the proposed road and railway. The stories confirmed that the contract had been signed with McKenzie & Mann in return for a grant of 25,000 acres of land to the contractors for each mile of track. To Glenora residents, the price seemed drastic. Only mining claims staked before June 15th would be recognized and protected by law from inclusion in the railway land grant. They had to get out into the bush and stake their claims before the deadline, or else McKenzie & Mann would get them all. Other details of the proposed contract ranged from wild stories to, occasionally, the truth. According to the contract, McKenzie & Mann would complete the railway by September 1st. The winter road was to run from the recently established post at Dewdney to the Teslin Lake outpost. The amount of money the company received changed with each storyteller, but certainly huge sums of money would change hands; one newspaper reported the sum of $250,000 as the first payment.

With the stories and rumours on the rampage, Jim Callbreath decided he could not pass up this chance to find his fortune, but, he promised himself, this time he would make money for sure. He would not be one of the foolish ones to head out into the wilderness to pan in some God-forsaken creek for gold. No, this time he would make money on the other side of the business. He offered any man in the place a good day's pay to appear at seven the next morning. He was going to build himself a hotel.

At seven sharp, Callbreath Construction began its first building. Jim and his crew started their task of converting his nondescript warehouse into a hotel. When Kate arrived at the store and saw the commotion, she became caught up in the idea and decided she too would become involved. Returning to her tent, she pulled her black leather bag from under her cot. From deep beneath the folds in the secret compartment she brought out the five dollar gold piece that Moses and Lou Brennan had given to her when she left Vancouver. It was her last bit of cash but she knew she had to take the gamble. Holding the precious money in her hand, she felt that this was her one chance at success. Jim Callbreath was never a man to turn down a good business proposition. After a brief discussion, he agreed to allow Kate some space in his new hotel. Her idea was a good one — a

Main Street, Glenora, May 1898.
The Glenora Hotel is the third building from the top left. (HJW/NAC)

restaurant would improve his venture. The partnership was struck, and Kate owned her first business, the Glenora Restaurant.

Within a few days, the sagging warehouse began to take on its new shape. The main building was a two-storey structure, 24' long by 16' wide. First, the crew turned the ground floor into a lobby of sorts, with a rough bar running the full length of the building. As well as its normal function, the bar also served as an office and registration desk. Then they made the upper floor into sleeping quarters. The so-called private rooms consisted of one large dormitory divided into small cubicles by partitions made from unplaned lumber. These partitions were only head high so that in winter the heat could circulate. Each "private room" resembled a bull pen and contained a double bunk made from the same rough lumber as the partitions. For the complete comfort of the guests, a straw tick graced each bunk. In less than a week, the packing shed attached to the south side of the erstwhile warehouse was miraculously converted into Kate's restaurant.

With her five dollar gold piece, she established a line of credit at Jim's store and bought the basic necessities. A few yards of green print, some white-wash, tin dishes, flour and sugar and she was ready for business. Jim added his *pièce de résistance* to the decor of the new establishment. Above the door of the new hotel swung a large white sign with black lettering: "Glenora Hotel and Restaurant — Now Open For Business." In small lettering at the bottom, the sign boasted: "Accommodations for 100 Guests." All Kate and Jim had to do was sit and wait for the ice on the Stikine to melt and the stampeders and railway men to flood into town.

The April rains began to soften the river ice, and every day Glenora watched anxiously for the first signs of breakup. Their life depended on the one vital act of nature. Wagers and gambling pools were made on the day, hour and minute the ice would move. An unusual cold snap in mid-April plunged the community back into winter. Glenora settled back in misery to wait again. Finally, on April 26, the thunder of cracking ice called the town to the river bank. Huge mounds of ice rocked and piled against each other, slowly at first, as the crowd watching the spectacle cheered with excitement. At last the great masses of ice broke free and rushed seaward, releasing Glenora from winter. The following day the river was clear above Glenora to Telegraph Creek. Jim had a contract with the Hudson Bay Company to take supplies to a logging crew, so he had to head upriver to check the trails. Many companies would be ready to pay top dollar to have goods packed over to Telegraph Creek and up to Teslin Lake, and Jim wanted to be the first on the spring trails. He left George Kelly in charge of the new hotel and Kate looking after her restaurant, confident that not much could happen in the week or ten days that he expected to be away.

It was another week before the river was free of ice below Glenora, and even then the strong current and high water made the river unsafe for steam navigation. So the people of Glenora waited and watched the river again. Finally, on May 7, the *Monte-Cristo* celebrated her arrival by blasting her whistle again and again. People from miles around came running to the shore as she proudly edged her way up to the Glenora wharf. The steamer was a sight to behold for those who had waited so patiently for supplies, mail and customers. She was the first of the fleet operated by the Canadian Development Company, a subsidiary of McKenzie & Mann, and her arrival heralded the economic boom that would spark the whole northern country. Along with the desperately needed food supplies, mail and machinery, the *Monte-Cristo* also brought staff for the new office of the Canadian Development Company and a full load of prospectors and explorers. The newcomers were filled with anticipation, excitement and questions. Where was the All Canadian Route? How many miles to Dawson? Where was the railway station? And the incessant Where do we dig for gold? The chaotic bustle was great fodder for the oldtimers making fun of the naiveté of the tourists.

The *Monte-Cristo* had steamed from Wrangell to Glenora in a record three days. The captain made his way to the new Glenora Restaurant and regaled the crowd with his experiences. On top of a difficult voyage, he had to stop for stranded travellers along the way. He picked up 75 men, but, being overloaded, he left behind at least a thousand more along the banks of the Stikine. The captain predicted that they would be picked up by the steamers that would soon follow the *Monte-Cristo.* He himself would return to Wrangell the next morning on a trip that, because of the current, would probably take less than a day. Somehow, the joy of the *Monte-Cristo*'s speedy round trip escaped those who had struggled for weeks to get to Glenora over the ice.

The Stikine River fleet grew daily as steamers, men and supplies moved up and down the river. The Canadian Development Company, true to their first promise, established regular service between Wrangell and Glenora. The advertisements in the Vancouver and local papers read: "*Victorian, Columbian, Monte-Cristo* and *Canadian*, leave daily from Wrangell for Teslin and Dawson — Steamers and boats now being built at Teslin." These advertisements were not actually false, in that the whole operation was planned; it was just unfortunate that construction was so far behind schedule that most of the route did not exist. Steamers arrived at Glenora daily to load and unload mail, machinery, lumber and a varied lot of passengers, all of them lured by the promise of an easy trail to the Klondike gold fields.

There were businessmen, railroad men, prospectors, government agents and tourists; men in rough work clothes, heavy-soled boots and weather-beaten hats and men in frock coats; and even a few ladies in afternoon dresses and hats. Together they trudged up and down the river bank (the town's main street), forming a continual parade for the Glenora natives.

Children caught up in the contagious excitement darted freely among the dunnage bales and piles of lumber, and the shantytown of tents and instant buildings was hide-and-seek heaven. A young boy ran past the crowds to the Glenora Restaurant.

"Miss Kate, I have a big one for you," he boasted, as he flung his string of fresh trout on the counter. Kate had commissioned the lad, Guy Lawrence, to supply the restaurant with fresh fish. In return, she paid him a penny and all the pie he could eat. What more could a young man of ten wish for? When Guy arrived with his catch, Kate instructed him to put the sign in the window. Proudly he took a stool and placed the menu sign in the front window: "Today's Special Fresh Trout." Just then, Guy glanced upriver and gave a shout for Kate.

"Miss Kate, here comes Mr. Callbreath, he's back. He sure will be surprised we have fish for supper, won't he!"

Coming out from the kitchen brushing flour from her hands, Kate remarked that Jim was going to be surprised by more than the fish.

Jim had been away from Glenora longer than he had expected. Now, as he rode his horse along the trail, he was certain that he had stepped out of time. Men rushed past him willy-nilly, ignoring him in their haste. Other men hauled lumber, while two men with loads on their backs stepped right in front of his horse. Off to the side of the trail eight more men were pegging out building lots with surveying equipment and stakes. In the cleared space, hundreds of tents were scattered at random and piles of stores covered every bit of ground. When Jim dismounted and started to walk his horse down the main trail, he was astounded to see the sign of another trading company operating out of a tent adjacent to his own store. The owners, John Shaw and Ed Tomilson, greeted Jim like an old friend and invited him to investigate their new tent store. They fairly bubbled over in their enthusiasm as they told him how they had just ar-

Yukon Field Force camp, Glenora, May 1898. (HJW/NAC)

rived a few days before from Tacoma, Washington, and sincerely appreciated renting his land. They quickly added that they had paid one month's rent in advance to George Kelly. Shaw and Tomilson represented the Fife-Alaska Company of Seattle, a reputable and well-established firm. They were elated at the business prospects of Glenora and the future of the north. They did, however, expect to leave for Dawson just as soon as the railroad was complete.

Leaving the Fife-Alaska Company, Jim encountered a family of tourists nonchalantly sunning themselves on a grassy spot outside a tent they had attached to the northeast corner of his own cabin. They waved to Jim as he walked past and invited him for tea. One scene of disbelief led to another as Jim arrived at the field he had ordered ploughed in his absence and found a complete newspaper outfit in full production. Tim Thompson, the energetic editor-publisher, was so delighted to meet the pioneer of Glenora that he immediately sold Jim a subscription and at the same time extracted a news story on the history of the town. But the most incredible scene still awaited Jim. As he turned a corner around his barn, he was confronted with three dray lines hauling supplies to a camp of soldiers bivouacked there. Jim fled back to Tim Thompson to demand some sort of explanation for the army installed in his back field. Thompson gave Jim the only answer he knew.

"Well I can't say for sure, Mr. Callbreath, just why the army is here, but when I went over for an interview, the colonel was very blunt and told me, 'The Yukon Field Force have been sent for the protection of the inhabitants, just in case any deep-draught Spanish Man-Of-War might stray up the Stikine and attack.' "

Jim sought refuge in Kate's restaurant, but the *Skagit Chief* had just docked. Kate was too busy to talk and could pass on only a few words as she hurried to serve the customers pouring into the dining room. But she did introduce her new helper, Miss Clara Corliss, who was running by with plates of stew. Kate offered Jim a cup of coffee which he accepted but waved away the plate of stew. He was so overwhelmed by the day's events that he was just too tired to eat, and he left for what he hoped would be the security of his own bed. The very next day, the first issue of the Glenora *News* chronicled Jim's adventures in the lead story, "The Town That Was Built In A Day."

> In the fortnight Jim Callbreath was away, the quiet town with a population of less than one hundred souls became a bustling city of more than 3,000 inhabitants, with a score of steamboats running to it, and two railroads projected and due to be built immediately or sooner. This is the Glenora of today.

Kate's restaurants in Glenora. Kate is standing in the centre, above, and on the left, below. (KMK)

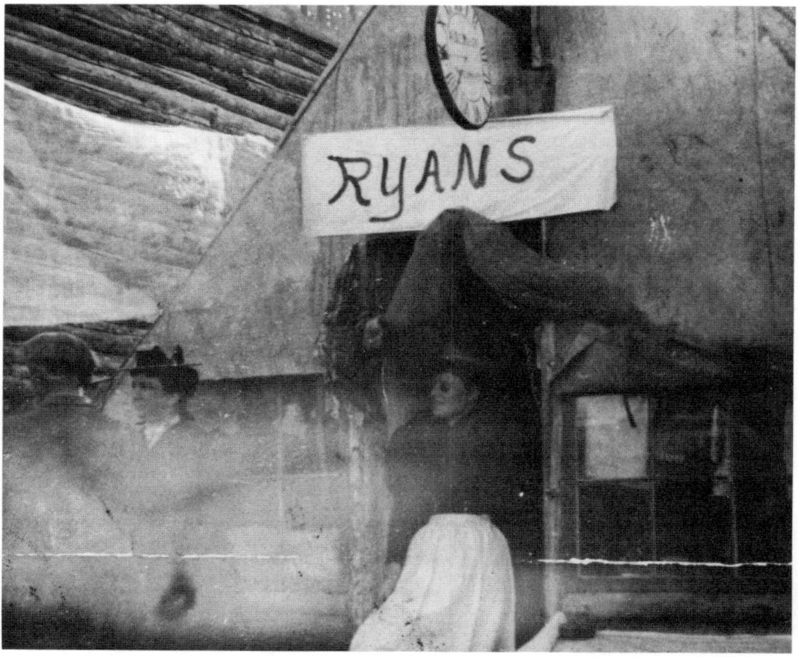

Summer in Glenora

Glenora bubbled with hope, enthusiasm and prosperity. Travellers and businessmen came and went. Some took the daily steamer that went upriver to Telegraph Creek, while others boarded the steamer bound downstream for Wrangell. With the Stikine River Fleet in full operation, Kate's restaurant prospered. Tim Thompson continued to publish editorials in the Glenora *News* extolling the advantages of travelling to the Klondike by the All Canadian Route: under British rule, the North West Mounted Police protected travellers from cut-throats and thieves, the laws of the land guaranteed contracts and no one would encounter the unfair tariffs and toll gates that dotted the Chilicoot and Dyea routes. Glenora grew at a phenomenal rate. New businesses sprang up as suddenly as the flowers of spring along the main street, a conglomeration that included, as well as Kate's restaurant, four outfitting companies, a butcher shop, two bakeries, a blacksmith shop, a barbershop, five hotels, a stationery store, six packing outfits and the first brewery in northern British Columbia. Early one June morning, Jim Russell, Dick Smith, Ben Wehfrita and Carl Zoelle arrived on the *Skagit Chief* and immediately began to build a 16' by 24' brewery. Their building contained six wooden vats, each capable of holding 360 gallons of beer. By the end of the second week in June, the four had the brewery constructed and the beer brewed. When the first batch went on sale, the thirsty consumers declared the new product the very best beer money could buy anywhere in Canada. Only three months earlier, a man did well to purchase enough flour to survive, and now he could buy anything his heart desired, including cold beer.

The packing outfits, operated by men of the trails who knew the country, were the economic backbone of the town. The main firms were owned by Charley Severance, Frank Mobley, Jim Callbreath and Charles Clearihue. Each had all the trade he could handle, and they remained friendly competitors. Rivalries among the outfitters were a kind of sport, each trying to make the fastest time or carry the biggest load. Charley Severance had 100 horses and about fifty men on the trails most of the time. He shared an office building with the Butler Co. of Montana. The Butler Co. represented mining investors, but as yet it had no mines in which to invest. In the next building, Mrs. Adele Bucholtz ran a laundry and Mrs. Bev DeVoe operated a bakery. Next to the bakery, Frank Mobley had the offices of his packing outfit while his wife operated another bakery and a confectionery store. When Pat Brennan arrived in Glenora from Vancouver, Kate sent him to Frank Mobley for a job in his store. No one willing to work went without a job, employers paid top wages and a strong young man with an honest face would be hired without further ceremony. Dominic Burns arrived in Glenora early in May and immediately established a permanent home and opened his business. His "tent butcher shop" was beside Frank Mobley's building, and as the new business people of Glenora formed their town, Kate and Dominic began a friendship that was to last for the rest of their lives.

The Reverend John Pringle pitched the tent in which he combined home and church on the end of the string of buildings that constituted the Glenora business district. Since his arrival in Glenora, Pringle had made himself known to everyone in the town and on the trail. He was a goodwill ambassador not only for his God and his church but for every other social organization. He travelled constantly up and down the trail between Glenora and Telegraph Creek, frequently walking the twelve miles to Telegraph Creek after breakfast and returning to Glenora for supper; he considered the twenty-four miles merely a brisk walk. Along the way, he assisted anyone who needed help in any way he could. Around Glenora, he encouraged the men as they worked and never hesitated to throw off his coat and lend a hand to put up a tent or pull a wagon out of the mire. On the trails and in the settlement, his reputation as a kind and considerate man grew, and many Glenora men turned to him in times of desperation. He made it his business to cultivate the acquaintance of every new person who came to town and invited all travellers to attend his church services. If anyone took the Lord's name in vain or beat his horse, Pringle delivered a sound lecture on the spot. Nor did the Reverend have any inhibitions

Reverend John Pringle preaching Sunday morning service to members of the Yukon Field Force at Telegraph Creek, July 30, 1898. (NAC)

about stepping into the bar at the Glenora Hotel or Carl Zoelle's brewery and inveighing against the sins of liquor, and soon the regulars dubbed him "the bar-room preacher." Nevertheless, the prospectors and packers liked the Reverend and respected him even when he rebuked them for their worldly deeds.

Every day, Pringle was in and out of Kate's restaurant, gathering information and passing along his greetings, and he soon became determined to coax Kate to his Sunday service. The Catholic church had strict rules against her attending Protestant services, but since there was no Catholic Church in Glenora, she and Miss Clara finally agreed to visit. They talked Dominic Burns and Charley Severance into escorting them. True to his word, Pringle gave his hell-fire and brimstone sermon. His visitors tried to keep their composure, but when the time came for the offering a haggard and unshaven prospector rose and passed his well-worn weather-beaten hat for the collection. Afterwards, the Reverend called the man aside, thanked him for his assistance and politely suggested that at future services perhaps a more respectable container could be found to collect for the Lord. The following Sunday, once again Kate and her friends attended, anxiously waiting to witness the prospector's choice of collections plates. On cue, the prospector rose and without so much as a blink of an eye he politely passed a long-handled miner's shovel in front of them for their donation to the Lord and Reverend Pringle.

The business life of Glenora grew peacefully enough, but the peace was only skin deep. With the discovery of gold in the Klondike, the unsettled Canada-Alaska boundary, which had previously seemed unimportant, became a burning issue. Both the Canadian and American governments were aware of the vast fortune now being unearthed in the north, and both would do everything in their power to gain control of the valuable land. Neither side would discuss their negotiations publicly, but as the conflict continued in Ottawa and Washington, the unrest of the American miners in the Yukon became a very real threat to the Canadians nominally in control. There was a realistic fear of open rebellion, and Yukon civil authorities dispatched secret documents to officials of the North West Mounted Police urgently requesting assistance.

Prime Minister Wilfred Laurier, a shrewd and calculating man, watched developments in the territory with apprehension. He knew the Yukon unrest could explode into battle. Directly following Clifford Sifton's report, Laurier called up a contingent of the Canadian Militia's Permanent Force, selected its most able leaders and placed under their command the new Yukon Field Force. He instructed the commander-in-chief, Colonel Theodore D. Evans, to leave for the Yukon as soon as humanly possible. Only Col. Evans and a few of his officers knew that they were going to the Yukon to curtail a rebellion, and they were under strict orders from the Prime Minister never to disclose the true purpose of their mission. The army consisted of 200 officers and enlisted men and represented every important militia unit in Canada; including 32 men from No. 4 Co., Royal Regiment of Canadian Infantry, Fredericton, New Brunswick.

Accompanying the force was a distinguished group of five women. Lady Aberdeen, the wife of the Governor General, had initiated the Victorian Order of Nurses the previous year and

Journalist Faith Fenton in her Yukon summer regalia. (NAC)

needed to win the support of the medical profession. She seized upon the good will of the Prime Minister to send her first team, four of her best nurses, into the Klondike to aid the miners. The fifth woman was the noted Toronto journalist Faith Fenton, assigned by the Toronto *Globe* to keep the Canadian public and the world up-to-date on the events on the All Canadian Route to the gold fields. The observant and articulate Henry Woodside, a Captain in the Canadian Cavalry and a native of Portage La Prairie, Manitoba, also kept written and photographic records on the All Canadian Route, although from the military perspective. An experienced writer, surveyor and photographer, he had come to the north earlier than the rest. He had attempted to go to the Klondike via the Chilicoot Trail, but he had been turned back. Waiting out the early months of the year in Wrangell, Henry attached himself to the Yukon Field Force in May and finally travelled up the Stikine River with them on the *Strathcona*. In his numerous articles published in the leading papers of the day, Henry heaped scorn on the treatment handed out to travellers in American territory, generating all the public support he could for the All Canadian Route.

The arrival of the Yukon Field Force in Glenora on May 14 caused more than excitement; it caused chaos. The soldiers camped in Jim Callbreath's back field caused a particular stir among the Glenora packers. The soldiers complied with military order and dressed in full military regalia, a style of life that contrasted sharply with the way the ordinary inhabitants of Glenora lived. The northern packer was by nature one of the most independent men under the sun and led a life of absolute and total freedom. His attitude to a job or an employer was indifference. If he thought a man straight, he would do his job well and without question, giving more than a full day's work for a day's pay and undertaking jobs that most would find unbearable. But if he was unhappy with the work or the boss, he would just move on with the breeze to the next place. Into the midst of this freedom came the Yukon Field Force, with all the Queen's own regulations. The initial curiosity and awe between the two groups soon turned to scorn. The Force hired the best packers to carry its supplies, but many a story was recited by the quiet, poker-faced packer who had gazed in wonder at "them salutin' fellers." The men of the mountains could not understand how a man could subject himself to such restrictions and live com-pletely devoid of self-direction. Their view of a man who would allow himself to be put to bed by a bugle and awakened by the same, who would walk through the bush sporting a full uniform, who would answer another man with a salute was not printable.

Aware of the need for harmony, Col. Evans sought the help of the Reverend John Pringle in breaking up the animosity between the two groups. Pringle had begun the habit of carrying the mail and Faith Fenton's reports between the camp and the store in town. On each trip he would shoulder his satchel filled with mail and small requests from the store and would return from the camp burdened with letters from the men to their sweethearts, wives and mothers. The nurses and Miss Fenton watched for his slender, muscular figure approaching the camp, and with a shout of welcome they would rush out to greet him. Both sides trusted Pringle, and this is why Col. Evans enlisted his aid. To end the feuding once and for all, they decided to organize a tremendous joint celebration of the Queen's Birthday on May 24.

Pringle acted as chief organizer and took responsibility for the townspeople. He and Henry Woodside had become friends, united by their love of politics, their Liberal connections and their strong advocacy of Prime Minister Laurier and Clifford Sifton. Henry planned the army's contribution, along with Faith Fenton. Tim Thompson advertised the event, and Kate recruited the women to prepare the picnic supper. When Henry had learned that Kate hailed from Johnville, New Brunswick, he had brought the nurses to supper at her restaurant, because one of

Victoria Day Celebrations in 1898. Kate appears on the right in this photo taken in the doorway of her Glenora restaurant. (KMK)

them came from nearby Woodstock; they helped organize the celebration, too. Ed Shaw took charge of the sporting events, and George Kelly gathered musicians from both groups.

The official events began at noon, when the Yukon Field Force, in full military regalia complete with white pith helmets, paraded down the main thoroughfare of Glenora. They marched to an open field prepared for the sports events, and when the parade dispersed, the army changed into civilian clothes. They battled the townspeople in a hotly contested ball game before the races and games. Social barriers melted as men and children competed in sack races, and packers and stampeders challenged soldiers in arm-wrestling and wood-chopping. Every cook in town competed with the army cooks and contributed their most tempting dishes to the sumptuous picnic supper. Each church group and every organization tried to outdo the others in providing the best treats. Henry Woodside took the opportunity to record history in the making, photographing the celebration from the bluff behind the makeshift fair grounds. The grand finale was a huge bonfire, around which town and camp gathered for a concert. Never to be outdone, John Pringle treated the group to humorous recitation, and George Kelly played the banjo, accompanied by two enlisted men on harp and accordion. As the evening shadows lengthened, the voices of Glenora and the Yukon Field Force united in song rose to the highest treetops.

The Queen's Birthday celebration ended the hard feelings between the Glenora residents and the Yukon field Force, but tensions of another kind soon mounted. Pringle's and Woodside's defense of the Canadian government brought them into outright conflict with the Americans who came to Glenora trying to lure stampeders to retrace their steps to Wrangell and go to the Klondike via the Skagway and Lake Bennett route. In a public letter published in the Glenora *News*, Woodside wrote, "The hardships over either of the northern routes are nearly as great as they are over the Stikine now, and I for one would say to all, don't be in too much of a hurry to turn back to the Dyea route. It simply would be out of the frying pan and into the fire." At the same time, the development of the All Canadian Route was not making enough progress to justify Woodside's and Pringle's faith. They were worried because construction had not begun on either the railway or the wagon road, and Henry had sent a telegram to Clifford Sifton urging him to tell them where construction plans stood. In their compulsion to get to the Klondike, hundreds of men had allowed themselves to be led far south of their destination by promises made by Canadian officials that the railway to Teslin and the steamer service on Teslin Lake would begin operating that summer. These officials could not imagine the natural barriers that faced the adventurers they had lured to Glenora and Telegraph Creek and stranded there. Taking the initiative, Woodside and Pringle fell into the habit of holding a supper meeting each night at Kate's restaurant. With careful optimism, they began to organize a meeting of all the prospectors in the district.

Every day brought more frustration for the stampeders waiting for some word on the construction of the railway. They had few choices. Some talked about taking a chance on following the Yukon Field Force to Teslin in the hope that they could obtain passage on the steamers that were supposedly being built there. Others considered returning downriver to Wrangell and facing the obstacles of the Chilicoot, despite Henry Woodside's warnings. Nearly all had their choices circumscribed by the lack of money and provisions. To make the tension even greater, the clear hot weather of early summer led to forest fires that appeared to threaten the town. No one could do anything to control the elements; they could only hope the fires would burn themselves out quickly. But the irritating smoke floated over the town and added to the unrest and distemper of the stranded prospectors. After a week, the rains came, relieving the town of the dense smoke and the danger of fire, but not of its social unease. When the smoke finally cleared, Henry Woodside climbed the bluff behind the town again and took photos of the town of Glenora bursting at the seams.

The appearance of Hank Freeman and his partner, the black James Booth, renewed the hope of the becalmed adventurers, because they had just completed a round trip from Glenora to Teslin Lake. Freeman and Booth were the very first non-natives to do this, and at last the sojourners had some first-hand information on the condition of the Teslin Trail. The two men had left Wrangell on the river ice in March. Heading up the Stikine River, they encountered all the hardships imaginable on a winter expedition. They survived their ordeal and arrived at the Teslin outpost after seven weeks on the trail, but Freeman's feet had been crushed on the ice and he was in poor condition. After two weeks of rest they felt ready to make the return trip to Glenora, where their employer, the Canadian Development Company, had set up an office. Together the men had packed 800 pounds of mail and supplies to Teslin, a godsend to the men stranded at the outpost. Freeman and Booth were instant heros when they arrived in Glenora. They repeated their stories again and again and were toasted and treated wherever they went. People were relieved to hear that crews were working on the Teslin Trail, and Freeman reported that the Donnelly Party was located around Spruce Mountain. A second crew was hard at work close to the Teslin outpost, and both of the road crews had sent urgent requests for supplies and men to work on the road. They also urgently requested that the Canadian Development Company pay them for the work that they had already completed. Freeman and Booth showed that all was not lost. A road was indeed being built, and it was possible to travel along the Teslin Trail from Telegraph Creek to the Teslin outpost. The pioneer of the Teslin Trail gave practical advice to anyone who would listen: "To travel north you have to figure 250 pounds for thirty days. Also it will take a man and two horses all summer to pack in enough supplies to Teslin to survive the winter." His advice, though bleak, was reasonable, and experienced packers realized that anyone contemplating the Teslin Trail should heed it. But during the summer of 1898, wise words were seldom heeded. Major events seemed to occur in an instant, and few took Hank Freeman's advice.

The Glenora *News* bolstered Freeman's reports that work on the road had started. It added the news that John Turner, the Premier of British Columbia, openly supported the wagon road and would do all in his power to see that it became a reality that summer. No route offered an easy way in — or out, for that matter — and each individual had to take the path he thought best. Continual reports of more gold discoveries in the Klondike and in northern British Columbia only piled hysteria on top of hysteria. In Glenora, Henry Woodside and John Pringle continued to badger government officials for action on the railway and the wagon road. They repeated telegrams to both Clifford Sifton, the federal Minister of the Interior, and Prime Minister Wilfrid Laurier. Frustrated by inaction, they called a public meeting for June 7 in front of the Kamloops Hotel. To everyone's surprise, more than a thousand stranded miners, prospectors and travellers gathered to vent their anger at the government. The meeting elected Henry B. Pullen-Berry as chairman and seven of the town's leading residents as his committee. They instructed this committee to draft a blunt letter to Premier Turner and took up a collection on the spot to send Captain Henry York downriver on the first steamer to deliver the letter in person to Victoria. This letter read:

> Sir:
>
> The construction of the recently commenced wagon road between Glenora and Teslin Lake having been suddenly abandoned, we the citizens and free miners, now located at Glenora and Telegraph Creek, have in public meeting assembled on this the 7 day of June 1898 and declared extreme dissatisfaction with the Government of the Dominion of Canada, in advertising in Europe and elsewhere, advocating the Stikine Route as the best possible road to the Yukon gold fields, with the completion of a wagon road from Glenora to Teslin Lake in the spring of the present year and;
>
> Whereas no pack trail is adequate for the transportation of goods waiting at Glenora and Telegraph Creek we pray that for the credit of British Columbia and the good of the Canadian route, your governments will take immediate action for the completion of the aforementioned wagon road.
>
> Whereas there are now from 2,000 to 3,000 miners stranded at Glenora and Telegraph Creek unable to proceed or return, we would respectfully urge upon your government the desirability and necessity of instructing your representatives here to act at once to employ these men on the work of completing the road to Teslin Lake.
>
> We beg to remain, Sir, H.B. Pullen-Berry, London England; Captain Henry Francis York, Telegraph Creek and Greenock, Scotland; I.M. Brayshaw, Victoria, B.C.; Edgar Haydon Searle, Glenora and Monmouthshire, England; Pat H. Brennan; Henry Woodside, Captain Canadian Cavalry; and Sidney Rattray Ashvale, Aldershot, England.

The signatories of the letter were clearly British subjects and men of authority, with a more-than-just complaint against the government of Canada. The men of Glenora saw Captain York off with handshakes and encouragement and settled back to wait for his return. But fate once again drew men into the Canadian interior. On June 10, the Glenora *News* reported a gold strike within two miles of Glenora. The town went wild. Edward Robinson brought Tim Thompson a sample that gave 75 colours to the pan, the largest twice the size of a pin's head. This did not represent a new Eldorado, but gold was gold, and where that was found there had to be larger deposits. Thompson put Robinson's pan as discovered on public exhibition at the Glenora *News* office so sceptics could see it with their own eyes. A telegraph message from Captain York reinforced the mood of jubilation: Premier Turner gave his word that the government of British Columbia would support the proposed wagon road.

But even as the Glenora residents applauded the efforts of Captain York and the work done by John Pringle and Henry Woodside, the staff of the Canadian Development Company received orders to shut down operations and began secretly moving their supplies back downriver. As rumour and contradiction continued to follow each other, the men called a second meeting for June 21. Henry Woodside, acting again as secretary of the meeting, drafted a resolution to Premier Turner demanding immediate action.

Meanwhile, in Ottawa, Clifford Sifton delivered one of the most dramatic speeches ever heard in the House of Commons. Sifton defended the choice of the Stikine Route and the proposed railway, citing the economic rewards that would be realized for all Canadians. As minister of the interior, he could envision the wealth of the new country and the tremendous benefit to his government. He spoke so eloquently that even the doubters were converted, and the bill providing for the construction of the Cassiar Railway easily passed the House of Commons. But Sifton's success was short lived. The Conservatives, believing they had stirred up enough public feeling to justify drastic action, killed the bill in the Senate, where they commanded a majority. Sifton was incredulous. He could not believe that the Senate would stop one of the most important agreements of the decade. To those who had waited so patiently in Glenora and Telegraph Creek, the final word came through the Glenora *News*.

The staunch defender and public voice of the All Canadian Route had to withdraw his support in disgust. "It makes a man wild," Thompson wrote, "when he realizes the possibilities of the All Canadian Route, and then contemplates the incompetent manner in which Canada's humanity's interests have been handled. Twenty years from now people will talk of the disgrace and tell of the government which led five thousand Argonauts into the wilderness by means of the use of the good name of the Dominion, and left them there stranded."

The Canadian Development Company officials received direct orders to quit their operations immediately and move men and supplies out on the next steamer. To the desperate miners there were no questions asked and no answers given concerning the rumoured $1,600,000 cash subsidy already paid to the company. Nor was any thought spared for the 4,000 men and women who had been coaxed into northern British Columbia with grand promises of a railway and a wagon road. This was the first of many business capers by "the King and the Duke," as McKenzie and Mann were nicknamed, and the whole affair was labeled far and wide as the "Stikine-Teslin Joke." The headlines in the Glenora *News* summed up the story. "McKenzie & Mann have quit and gone to Kootenay. It's a damn shame. There is some crooked work being done. You can count on it."

Kate outside her tent with Reverend John Pringle. (KMK)

The Teslin Trail

The news of a second major gold strike at Twoya Creek spread like a brush fire. The small creek joined the Stikine River about thirty miles from Telegraph Creek. When the news of the strike hit Glenora, packers, contractors, salesmen, loggers, miners and tourists all hit the trail as if their life depended on it. By late afternoon on Saturday, July 9, the rumours gained credibility because of the ominous secrecy surrounding some miners seen "grubbing up" at Callbreath's store. Some had actually sneaked out of town. Early Sunday morning, groups stood on every corner piecing together fragments of news. By noon everyone was convinced that the discovery was indeed genuine, and the sudden arrival of a young man on horseback shouting "Gold in Twoya Creek" emptied John Pringle's church service.

Late that afternoon, as Kate sat outside her tent enjoying the warm July afternoon, Jim Callbreath rode past and called to her, "Got it like the rest, Kate. Take care of everything, see you in a couple of weeks."

The professional packer who vowed he would never again be infected by "gold fever" had caught it in spite of himself. Off into the wilderness he went, seeking the elusive gold with the keys of the hotel and the storeroom in his pocket. Across the street, Kate could see her neighbour Dominic Burns nailing a sign to his door. With a wave of his hand, he too was off, joining the string of men and horses heading along the trail. Kate went across to inspect the sign: "Closed — Gone To Twoya Creek — Back In Two Weeks." Men and animals paraded out of town all afternoon. John Pringle stopped by and declared his intentions to head up the trail, too. When Kate inquired if the "fever" had caught him, he laughed and told her he was going to Telegraph Creek and up to Teslin to test the trail. He guaranteed he would be back; he would not be lured by the sight of gold. He wanted to take in some supplies, because he intended to move forward toward Teslin before the winter set in, and he was one of the few people who would heed the advice of Hank Freeman. Before leaving, however, he wanted to square his restaurant bill with Kate.

"Put your money away, Reverend Pringle," Kate admonished him. "You're always a welcome guest in my place, and never a penny will you pay."

Her generosity surprised him, but Pringle knew it would be useless to refuse such a gift. With a handshake, a fond farewell and a promise to meet again soon, he prepared to leave.

"Sure, you don't think I'm going to sit here while everyone else is heading out, do you?" Kate blurted. "Why, I've sold my share to Baker Booth, and just as soon as I can get my provisions together I'm heading up the Teslin Trail."

The summer of 1898 had brought both discontent and exhilaration to Kate and the community of Glenora, and the Klondike continued to tease and torment with wild stories of enormous gold finds. The last news story they heard reported that $9,500,000 in gold bullion had been shipped out of the Yukon during the summer months. Stories of fortunes won and lost in a matter of hours spread, and the Klondike continued to draw Kate like a magnet. She completed the sale of her restaurant to Baker Booth and came away with a good profit for her summer's work. She sent back to Vancouver the $5 gold piece Moses and Lou Brennan had given her, proudly adding a profit to their investment. Financially secure once again, she went to the Hudson Bay outpost for a new outfit for the trail ahead.

Rumour of another major strike in the Atlin district surfaced in August and was confirmed by the Glenora *News*. The Commissioner of the Yukon, William Ogilvie, stated that the Atlin strike was "no fake," either, and that he was certain the new find could be an even greater discovery than the Klondike. This report sent the remaining men in Glenora rushing off to Atlin Lake. The Atlin discovery near the British Columbia-Yukon border offered a reasonable destination for those in the Stikine country. The obvious route was to head up to Telegraph Creek, up the Teslin Trail to Teslin City, and branch off westward to follow the Indian trail to Atlin. The adventurous spirits in Glenora considered the Atlin trip little more than a Sunday jaunt — that is, until they were on the trail.

In early September, Miss Clara took the steamer to the coast for a short holiday, and she and Kate planned to meet in the Yukon. After Clara's departure, Kate gathered her provisions and started on the trail to Telegraph Creek. The trail between Glenora and Telegraph Creek followed the winding Stikine upstream along its bank, and in spite of her aching muscles after her first day on horseback, Kate found the trip an adventure. A holiday spirit filled the warm September afternoon, as the stampeders who lined the trail shouted back and forth offering advice and encouragement to one another. They all felt certain they were finally on the right path to success. Nearing the settlement of Telegraph Creek in the late afternoon, Kate's horse suddenly pulled up shy. Both she and the horse were thrown off balance by a huge cable swinging over their heads. The packer who came alongside to see if she was all right told Kate the story behind the eerie wire floating high in the wind.

In the early 1860's, a plan was devised to connect the continents with a line of telegraph wires stretching from Seattle through British Columbia into the Yukon and over to Russian America (later Alaska), and thence across the Bering Strait and all the weary way around Siberia. In 1864, the British Columbia colonial assembly passed a bill approving the Russian-American Telegraph, and in August of that year Charles S. Bulkley, the newly appointed engineer-in-chief, ordered work to begin. During the next few years, Bulkley's men fanned out around the North Pacific. In a concentrated effort, the crews erected poles and strung wires from Alaska down through the Yukon. In October, 1867, just as they reached the mountain stream where Kate now stood, they received the news that the directors of the Western Union Company had cancelled the Russian-American Telegraph. Construction stopped at once. The men working on the lines believed they were halting only for the winter months; they did not realize that the venture was doomed and the wires were now obsolete. The Trans-Atlantic Cable had been laid successfully, and Western Union could now speed telegraph messages between the continents without the expensive and complicated Russian-American Telegraph. When the crew abandoned the site, they gave the spot its name: Telegraph Creek. Kate eased her horse past the skeleton poles as the wires waved at her, a ghostly reminder of man's struggle for advancement.

The Stikine River extended far inland beyond Telegraph Creek, but the community was the stopping point for navigation. Above Telegraph Creek, the Stikine flowed through narrow canyons down which the river swirled and eddied with a tumultuous rush. Even the most skilful Indian guide could not navigate the mighty river beyond Telegraph Creek. The Canadian Navigation Company steamboats stopped at the Telegraph Creek landing, and here the Teslin Trail officially began its 150-mile route through bush and muskeg to the next tiny outpost, Teslin City.

Telegraph Creek boomed and bustled during the summer of 1898. As in Glenora, government offices opened in Telegraph Creek, the Hudson Bay store expanded, mining companies from the United States and Canada set up offices, and the Yukon Field Force established a base camp there. The transportation of the Yukon Field Force and their supplies engaged over 400 animals and 50 packers, which in itself brought a surge in the economy of the outpost. Gold was being discovered sporadically in small deposits near Twoya, and the prospectors continued to invade the Cassiar district. They extracted just enough gold to lure more men into the country. When Kate first arrived in Telegraph Creek, a bulletin on the news board read, "washups $15 a pan." This represented good pay for a day's work, certainly enough to keep the gold rush going. The second bit of news was that Nellie Tashman had arrived in town the day before, having come down from the Cassiar country. Nellie was already a Cassiar legend. Older than Kate, she was well known as a pioneer and "the Mother of the North." Kate had heard many stories about Nellie's travels and hastened to meet a woman of such great courage. The meeting was a memorable occasion for both women. They had many friends in common, they had travelled the same trails, and both were independent businesswomen grateful for each other's existence. An instant rapport sprang up between Kate and Nellie, for they shared a pioneer spirit, the love of nature and the need to be free. They talked of books, friends, the Field Force, the search for gold and the beauty of the country around them. Kate spent two days with Nellie, discussing the past and speculating on the future. When Nellie boarded the steamer and

Kate bid her new friend good-bye, they both knew that although they took different trails they would meet again.

The North West Mounted Police constable stationed in Telegraph Creek made the rounds daily to caution anyone going into the bush. Each must be responsible for his own survival. All were warned that there was no guarantee they would find game and that they must carry enough food to keep them for some time. Posters everywhere warned travellers of the dangers awaiting them once they left the outpost. Inspector Primrose expanded his base camp at Dewdney and had renamed the boundary camp the Stikine Post. He came up to Telegraph Creek on the steamers at least twice a month, and more often if he was needed. He had known no rest that summer and fully realized the burden of responsibility on his shoulders. His custom had been to stop and eat at the Glenora Restaurant to say hello to Kate. His appearance on the upriver steamer at Telegraph Creek caused Kate to ask him if there was trouble. Primrose laughed at the sight of Kate, now operating her restaurant out of her tent in Telegraph Creek, and he joked that he had to come upriver for pie since she was no longer in Glenora. Primrose remained his usual secretive self as he tucked into the big piece of apple pie Kate had served him.

"No trouble that I can see, Miss Kate, your pie is as good as ever. I am just looking the situation over as the newspaper reports in Ottawa and Washington tell about starving miners here in the Stikine country. I thought it rather funny as I sit here eating the best pie in Canada."

The news shocked Kate, and she urged Primrose for more details. It was indeed true that numerous reports to government officials told of mass starvation in the Stikine and Dease Lake country, but, as far as those in the area could find out, there seemed to be lots of food, at the present time anyway. On the other hand, there was news of a group from Ashcroft, British Columbia, heading through the interior of the province and expected to arrive soon in Telegraph Creek. Primrose had received orders to find the party and report immediately on their whereabouts and condition. Primrose had been in Telegraph Creek only two days when the appearance of James Deacon gave proof of the hardships brought on by the foolhardy schemes some men tried in their lust to get to the Klondike gold fields. Primrose invited Deacon over to Kate's restaurant for a hearty meal and a friendly chat.

Deacon was an advance scout. The provincial government had hired him and his crew to guide a party of businessmen anxious to establish an alternate route through the interior of the province to the Klondike. Canadian goods and supplies could be carried over this route without any contact with Americans. The officials that had organized the Ashcroft party had chosen a complex route that began at the southern end of the province in Ashcroft and headed due north through the Rocky Mountains, the most difficult terrain in all of Canada. Deacon himself was a veteran of the bush. He cared little about how or where the government sent him as long as he was paid in advance (which he was), and he had started out by blazing a trail along the Old Caribou Road. The Caribou Road led the party to Quesnelle, and Deacon began blazing the new trail, expecting the main party to follow it. Leaving Quesnelle, Deacon had taken a rough trail to Hazelton, where he had rested for a couple of days while he waited for word from the main party behind him. The advance party then headed due north again with the compass set for Telegraph Creek. Deacon estimated that the main Ashcroft group consisted of 500 men and approximately 1,000 animals, a strange collection of beef cattle, pack mules, several hundred horses and a few cows. Deacon sent scouts back at intervals in the first days, but as the trail became more difficult his main concern was their own survival. They followed the river from Hazelton for 100 miles until they faced a mountain that demanded a climb of three miles. The descent led them to the Skeena River, a welcome relief. They followed the river until it diminished into the headwaters of the Nass River, and the Nass crossed the LePau Range, which was, as Deacon said, "the serious part of the journey." Deacon and his crew then faced the bold slate face of a mountain that reached a height of 5,000 feet and was never free of snow. They crossed the summit in June through ten feet of soft snow. Once on the descent, Deacon said, he and his men considered the rest of the trail through virgin forest and bog "the easy part of the trip." He estimated the distance they had covered between Ashcroft and Telegraph Creek at about 950 miles, through the most difficult county that nature had ever created.

The arrival of the Ashcroft scouting party stirred up a great deal of excitement in Telegraph Creek. In spite of Deacon's harrowing tales, everyone believed that now, with the trail blazed and the support of the provincial government assured, the cattle and supplies would arrive in a matter of days. It also seemed that a direct route had finally been established through Canadian territory.

Deacon arrived in Telegraph Creek feeling somewhat optimistic about the next stage of his trip, but he was chagrined when he found the Teslin Trail much like the trail he had just left behind. He was among those who had expected to find a railroad station and a train waiting to take him the rest of the way to the Klondike gold fields. While the community waited for the main Ashcroft party to arrive, reports began to come in from outside of the horrific ordeals of the men and animals that had tried to make their way through the northern Canadian wilderness. The full story of the Ashcroft Route took months to piece together. Many who began the journey never saw a mine, let alone a piece of gold; they were just grateful to escape with their lives. The main group of the Ashcroft party made it as far as the Nass River, but by that time they had exhausted their supplies. Before they left, the editor of the Ashcroft paper, Dr. John Reynolds, had advised the inexperienced men, "Do not burden yourselves with too many provisions as you will make it through to Telegraph Creek in thirty days, maximum." By the time they realized their bad judgement, returning was as daunting a prospect as going forward. They were stranded. After two months at the head of the Nass River, not knowing what they faced ahead, they built rafts on which to float downstream to the coast at Fort Simpson. With luck, they reached their goal, and from the beach they signalled for help to the steamers on the Pacific coastal route. Once the starving and disgusted men reached civilization, they alerted the authorities to the misfortunes of the Ashcroft party. Other steamers were immediately dispatched to pick up the remainder of the stranded men that followed behind. Of the group that left Ashcroft, a few stalwart men and a handful of cattle made it through to Telegraph Creek in August. When the poor thin scraggly creatures staggered into town, Dominic Burns offered top dollar for the meat. He promptly butchered the animals and advertised the best steak in northern British Columbia at exorbitant prices. In Kate's restaurant the special for the day was "Ashcroft Steak." The fate of those who had tried the Ashcroft route was a grim reminder of the dangers in the bush.

As Kate prepared for the next stage of her adventure, she was cautious of her own supplies, aware that what she carried would probably have to keep her for many months. Indian summer lingered in the Stikine country, putting the residents in a contented frame of mind. They had prospered that summer, crews were still at work on the Teslin Trail, and rumour had it that the Donnelly Company had received a contract to widen the road bed to four feet. The morning that Kate finally mounted her horse to begin her journey along the Teslin Trail, geese in their V formation flew above her, honking their respects as they left the Stikine country for a warmer climate. She could not help but wonder about her own sanity as she turned her horse north toward her next destination, Teslin City.

The tall woman on horseback leading a string of pack horses cut an unusual figure even on the Teslin Trail. Without concern for propriety, Kate had fashioned for herself a culotte-style riding skirt made of tough material so that she could ride in comfort. Her mackinaw was still in good condition, so she had just shortened it to make it comfortable to wear on horseback. Her one piece of femininity was the hat she wore constantly, which she christened her "cow breaker." This broad-brimmed straw creation decorated with a small spray of blue flowers tucked into its wide band became Kate's symbol and her lucky charm. It shaded her on hot days and kept her dry in the rain; with it, she fanned a stubborn fire or shooed away the flies. And it flattered her, too; her hair, still untamed, escaped from her bun to frame her soft face in wisps of fine curls. The first day on the Teslin Trail, Kate made the steep climb to the Indian burial ground twelve miles north of Telegraph Creek and 4,000 feet above the Stikine River. A sacred place for the natives, the white intruders called this spot simply "The Summit." The panorama alone made

Pack train animals being unloaded. (KMK)

the day's ride worth Kate's effort, in spite of her aching muscles and shortness of breath. As soon as the sun disappeared, she climbed into her sleeping bag under the trees.

Experienced packers had set the rules and timetable of the trail years before, and a tenderfoot soon learned to follow them. Rising time was three a.m. Breakfast was the most important meal of the day, so the fire was stirred and a kettle boiled for coffee and oatmeal, both to be laced amply with coarse brown sugar and thick canned milk. After breakfast, the animals were packed. Packing was considered a true art, and great care and consideration had to be given to the beasts of burden. A good cayuse (a name most often used for the green pack mules used on the Teslin Trail) could carry 150-200 pounds, depending on the skill of the packer. The more experienced packers would use only the cayuse, but Kate was hesitant. When she bought her animals at Glenora, she chose three cayuses to carry supplies and one good riding horse for herself. Charley Severance had schooled Kate in the art of packing, and now she was about to test her lessons. With a firm and steady hand, she placed a folded blanket over the back of each animal and secured it with a surcingle. Over the blanket she strapped an aparejo, a pack-saddle made of stuffed leather. Then she laid a tie rope over the saddle rigging and secured it all with a broad canvas cinch under the animal's belly. The tackle in place, she used a firm diamond hitch to tie on the canvas bags containing the load. No cayuse would tolerate a box on its back, and sensible packers would not risk injuring their animals by trying to make them carry boxes. With the packs in place, Kate stepped back to give each cayuse lots of room to see if she had achieved a good fit. The ears told the story. If she had done a good job, the animal would settle down after two or three twitches of his ears and legs. If not, he would let her know with the full vent of his fury. Packs and goods would scatter as he kicked and bucked with all his might, distributing not only his burden but any packer who happened to be standing in the way. But Kate knew horses and had been taught packing by an expert. With a little luck she and her string could hit the trail at five o'clock.

Once in motion, Kate kept up a steady, slow pace all day. No packer even considered stopping for any reason for six or seven hours. The cayuses trudging along the Teslin Trail took on the personality of the men for whom they worked — contrary and independent. Packers took only "cinch belt" lunches, because once the animals in a pack train stopped, they would never start again that day. Kate and her pack train meandered uphill and down, over corduroy bridges, through miles of burnt land etched with the tall black victims of the summer's fires, disturbing the silence of the forest with shouts of "Hoy, hoy" and the tinkling of the packer's bell on the lead horse. The Nahlin River crossed the trail again and again, its crystal water newly escaped from the mountain snow, and every time, woman and animals waded through the cold, swift water and clambered up the bank without stopping. Government crews had built a corduroy bridge across the Tahltan River and a second bridge spanned the creek above the first Hudson Bay post.

Kate rested at the post for a day and learned about a sixty-mile stretch of bunch grass just up the trail. She soon discovered what that meant: the horses insisted on stopping to feed every few feet. The tall grass also proved to be a haven for vicious mosquitoes twice as big as any Kate had ever seen before. Their persistence was the only force that could move the horses forward. Kate struggled through that grass and muskeg for three days before the trail returned to the security of timber growth.

At the end of her tenth day on the trail, Kate had almost reached the McDougall Camp when a traveller came upon her bivouac. She had just built her fire when he appeared, and trail hospitality demanded the sharing of the campfire. The man dismounted without hesitation, and Kate offered him a plate of supper. He introduced himself simply as Murphy, and as he came forward he offered the largest and possibly the dirtiest hand she had ever seen. Undaunted, she gripped the offered greeting in a firm handshake. He seemed to be travelling light, and told her he was on a return trip with mail and some gold from the post at Teslin City. He appeared friendly and cheerful, but Kate looked him over carefully before making a judgement. He towered over her own six-foot height, and she guessed that his dry, sunburned skin had not seen soap or a razor since spring. Trying his best to play the gallant knight of the trail, he admitted he had been on the look out for her for a few days. The communication system of the Teslin Trail rivalled the most modern telegraph system, and Kate's whereabouts were carefully monitored. Murphy rested himself against his saddle and began to relay the current gossip and trail conditions. He confessed that he had met a friend of hers earlier who had asked him to offer any assistance she might need. He went on to tell how he had slowly passed this tall gangly chap riding an equally skinny horse.

"I asked this fellow how the God damned son of a bitch of a trail was anyway? He gave me a queer answer. 'Just the way you described it, Sir,' and off he went. Yep, that's what he said, 'Just the way you described it, Sir.' Imagine that! He call me 'Sir.' I think it was the first time anyone ever called me 'Sir.' "

After a moment's reflection, Murphy added, "He hollered back for me to keep an eye out for Kate Ryan, and I guess that'd be you, ma'am?"

Kate responded to Murphy's story with a fit of laughter. "You, sir, have just met the Reverend John Pringle."

Murphy continued his monologue about the events of the trail. He peppered his speech with profanity but with no thought of offence to the listener. His coarse manner was kind; he knew no life but the woods and he wished for nothing different. He praised Kate for her ability to handle the horses and be on her own in the bush.

"Why, ma'am," he said, "you're as handy to have around as a klootchman. A klootchman's worth five dollars a day to any man out in these parts."

Recognizing this as a business offer as well as a compliment, Kate declined gracefully, but the trail life was a lonesome life, and Murphy, grateful to have someone to talk to, settled down for a good visit. Yarn followed yarn. As he told her about the time he packed a sick man in, waited while he died, and packed the corpse out again, all without getting paid, Murphy honoured her femininity by smoothing out his rough speech as best as he could. Kate smiled as he launched into his story about Windy Bill's baby, but she didn't let on that she had heard it already. Murphy had entertained Faith Fenton with it, and now Kate heard it first-hand.

"I ain't much on babies, but I helped to get one ready for christnin' onct," Murphy boasted. "My sister down east had sent me some poker chips, yeller plated ones, all shiny. Mrs. Bill, she took quite a likin' to them, and one day Bill came to me an' said that if I didn't mind selling them he'd like to have 'em. 'My woman thinks they'd be nice to fix up the youngster for christnin',' says he. So I made him a present of them. Mrs. Bill sewed 'em on a red shawl, made it all sort of spangled, and darned if that baby wasn't christened in a frock of poker chips. Bill was pleased as a fiddler. 'Bet he'll make a slick hand at the cards when he grows up,' he says."

Like the other men of the north, Murphy was confounded by the Yukon Field Force. As for his employer, he could offer only faint praise for the Hudson Bay Company even though he expected he would be able to go out at the end of the season with a good size roll. Kate was curious to know where "out" was exactly and whether he had any notion of heading to the Klondike gold fields. Murphy was not a miner and did not desire the material riches of the world. He told Kate he could have gone with his partners earlier in the summer into the Dease Lake Country, but as he tried to tell them all, there was no gold there, just fool's gold, and they were fools to go looking for it.

"They're all coming back from the Dease sick and starving to death," he added. "Damned fools came all the way from Edmonton with no idea how to survive in this godforsaken country."

Kate had to admit he was right. This was a fool's game for those who came to make a fortune when they knew nothing of the wilderness and had no idea even of how to stay alive. When the fire began to die down, Kate had to stop the flow of yarns and get some sleep. As usual, her day would begin at three a.m. Her guest pulled out his own bed roll, and he too retired for the few short hours until daybreak. He was up and ready for the trail early, and in spite of his rough manner, Kate felt sorry to see her new friend leave.

The new day brought a return from the forest to more muskeg. But the trail was a delight for the lover of nature. The forest abounded in wild flowers, and small animals unfamiliar with the scent of man would bound away from the streams at the sound of her packer's bell. Small creatures scurried under bushes to watch the invader from a safe distance. The gold of autumn coloured the trees, and at times Kate felt as if she were the only person in the world. She would greet another traveller or someone else's camp with a shout, but her pack train moved doggedly onward. Hundreds of prospectors, explorers and packers were scattered throughout the Stikine-Teslin country during the summer and fall of 1898. Few considered themselves pioneers, yet by their struggle they opened up a whole new part of the northern expanse. The Nahlin River crossed the Teslin Trail near Harry Harrison's saloon, but Kate decided to cross upriver instead of at the junction. Hank Freeman had warned her that Harrison had enough whisky to sink a good battleship and was inordinately fond of women. In Glenora, Freeman had reported that after he had sampled a few jolts of Harrison's notorious whisky, his own trip south had been shortened by a number of miles. Wary of Harry, his saloon and his reputation, Kate circled the trail and crossed the Nahlin River five miles upstream.

The weather stayed dry, although the nights turned very cold. Kate's spirits remained high. Each day her steady pace brought her nearer and nearer to Teslin City. She crossed the bubbling streams with their Indian names: the Tahltan River, the Twoya and at last the Teslin. The Teslin River emptied into Teslin Lake, and the outpost was located on the southern side of the lake. A navigation system on this waterway was to be the centre leg of the All Canadian Route to the Klondike, and boats were supposed to be operating from Teslin City to the Yukon until freeze-up. Kate was determined to get to Teslin City in time to catch the steamer; with good luck she would be in the Klondike by winter.

Winter in the North

T*eslin City* was reputed to be a "warm number" by the packers and miners who had seen the gambling and other disreputable goings-on there during the previous summer. Kate's first impression was no different. She arrived late in the afternoon and immediately set up her tent on the lake shore and built her fire before the sun went down. With the setting of the sun, heavy clouds settled in over the mountains, and before Kate could get the animals fed, the clouds opened up. The rain fell in sheets, while the tent door flapped so hard in the wind that, for awhile, Kate feared it would tear off. The rain never let up the next day or the next. It fell in constant torrents, making the whole country bleak and dismal. On the third day, Kate finally ventured to the outpost store, where the owner told her that the trail over which she had just travelled had turned into an impassable quagmire of mud and ruts.

Everyone gathered in the store discussed the Teslin Trail, and all doubted that there would be any more travelling over it until freeze up. The rain persisted for ten days. All movement along the lake ceased, and Kate had little choice but to stick close to her tent and try to maintain a fire. Finally on the eleventh morning she woke to birds twittering in the trees and horses plodding along the beach. A bright sunrise greeted her for the first time since she had arrived at Teslin City, but the sudden drop in the temperature had caused shell ice to form around the shore. Winter had sneaked in during the night. Kate's neighbours began to emerge from their tents and shacks, building fires and bundling up supplies. The men of camps such as this seemed to ignore the signs of winter as they went about their chores. They moved from place to place at whim, panning gold in one stream and then moving on to another, as if they expected to trip over life's fortune at any moment. Kate stirred her fire and, after a good hot breakfast, she attended to the animals. When she finished her work, she paid another visit to the outpost store to read the bulletin with the day's news. The major event of each day was the posting of the most recent gold find. Kate learned from the prospectors loitering about the store that during the previous summer the best find in Teslin City was "five colours to the pan, three of which would rattle." With such trifles Mother Nature continued to entice the stampeders further and further into the wilderness.

The history of Teslin City was short. In the spring of 1898, it was a rough and tumble camp which boasted two wooden structures. By July of the same year the "city" had grown to fifteen wooden buildings, with an overflow of tents clinging along the lake. The resident population was approximately fifty and the number of transients changed daily. Supplies were practically non-existent. What could be purchased sold for whatever price the seller wanted to ask. Basic food, such as flour and buckwheat, went for $1 a pound when available, while tobacco, sugar, salt or baking powder were such luxuries that they were rarely for sale at any price. To ease the hardships of northern life, however, whiskey flowed abundantly at several saloons for 50¢ a jolt. In Teslin City it was understood that an individual was responsible for his or her own survival. Money, even gold dust, was of no use to buy food. The town lived by a motto posted at the store: "A man must have his own food to get work; because a man cannot not live by work alone."

At the beginning of July, the first contingent of the Yukon Field Force arrived, and Col. Evans established a staging area on the lake shore that he named Camp Victoria. When the main contingent reached Teslin City, they received a terrible setback when they discovered that there were no steamers to take them the rest of the way to the Yukon. The Canadian Development Company had contracted to build several steamers to carry travellers along the All Canadian Route to the Klondike gold fields, but, because of the distant location and the lack of leadership and direction, very little had been accomplished. True to the first part of their obligation, McKenzie & Mann had built a small sawmill on Teslin Lake. An industrious labourer was guaranteed full time work and top wages as long as he had his own food, but most of the transients did not stay on the job very long because there was always a new gold strike to lure them away. McKenzie & Mann had started working on the first steamer, which they had named the *Anglian*, when the Yukon Field Force arrived. Colonel Evans immediately commandeered that steamer and set his men to help with the construction; at the same time, he had Major D.D. Young, his second in command, organize the building of enough boats to carry the main body of the Force in case the *Anglian* alone could not transport them all to the far end of Teslin Lake before freeze-up. The contract to build the *Anglian* was only a small part of the agreement between the government of Canada and McKenzie & Mann. That boat was to be the first of a fleet of steamers that would open up the waterways of the north. But when word finally reached Teslin City that the Senate in Ottawa had defeated the government bill, construction ceased, and by the time Kate arrived at Teslin City navigation on Teslin Lake had stopped for the winter.

A sense of urgency surrounded the transient settlement on Teslin Lake as fall began to set in. Those who were stranded were anxious to leave by any means possible, but the rains that followed Kate into Teslin had complicated transportation of all kinds, and the experienced packers agreed that it would be foolish to attempt any travelling until the snow came and allowed them to use dog sleds. Hugh Madden, whom Kate had known in Glenora, stopped by her camp. He acknowledged that he was in a poor way, low on funds and low on supplies. He wanted to beat a hasty retreat to Telegraph Creek, where at least he had money waiting in the mail. He offered to trade Kate his dog sled and three dogs for her horse and pack animals. Considering Kate's present position, it was a logical trade. She could not feed the horses during the winter and they would be useless for travelling. With a dog team, Kate hoped she could travel again when the snow came.

An outfit sponsored by a conglomerate of Quebec businessmen and led by a young coureur-de-bois had reached Teslin City a few days ahead of Kate. They were aghast to discover that no steamers plied the lake. Like many others, they had struggled so hard to get to the lake because they expected that, once they arrived, they could float down the river to the Klondike. They could scarcely believe that there were no boats. The leader himself cut a dashing figure. Tall and handsome, he carried himself well, and his knowledge and self-assurance gained him respect in the camp. He made himself known to everyone, and although he was cheerful in spite of his setback, he made it plain that he had no intention of spending the winter in Teslin City. One way or another, he was going to move on when the chance came. Kate, too, waited as patiently as she could. She could not open her restaurant because supplies were too meagre, but her nursing skills were in constant demand.

Earlier that fall, John Pringle had travelled as far as Atlin, and in October he sent word with an Indian scout that Kate should join the Atlin group at the first opportunity. Certainly Pringle was concerned for her safety, but he was also in desperate need of her medical ability in the Atlin camp. Considering Pringle's request, Kate approached the energetic leader of the Quebec party with a business deal he could not refuse. If he would take her and her supplies over to Atlin, she would give him her dog team and sled. For the stranded coureur-de-bois, owning a dog team meant transportation, and he jumped at the chance to leave Teslin City. Kate realized that Atlin would not be any better than Teslin, but at least she was wanted there, and she would have a head start next spring. Looking around the bleak lake shore, she knew that nothing could be much worse than spending the winter where she was. In late November Kate and her companion finally set out for Atlin. The thermometer read -40° the first night and sank to -60° on the third night, but Kate later reported that they had been "very lucky" because they had not had to face what she feared the most, heavy snow storms. It was sixty miles from Teslin City to Atlin over one of the most difficult mountain trails in all of the Canadian northwest. They reached Atlin on the fifth day, and the whole camp welcomed them with a great celebration. Kate felt that she had returned home, for among the welcomers were Reverend Pringle and Dominic Burns. They and other friends from Glenora helped Kate to establish herself in her own place, a 12' by 14' tent. It had no floor, but it did have the luxury of two windows, for which she had paid a fabulous sum in Teslin City. Later, she rented those same windows to a watchmaker for $10 a month. As well as nursing the sick, the job for which John Pringle had summoned her, Kate took in washing, and she also reopened her restaurant, sometimes using her own supplies but often using the supplies brought to her by men unskilled at doing their own cooking.

In December 1898, Atlin consisted of a few log structures, a number of tents braced and covered with fir branches, some oddly constructed shanties which were habitation for both men and animals, and one roughly built wooden frame building that served as the store, post office, way house, hospital and anything else necessary. The pioneers stranded in Atlin during the long winter huddled against the cold and snow, dependent on each other for survival. But Kate's enthusiasm for Christmas was not to be dampened, and she organized a community celebration that would reach out to everyone in the camp. People made small gifts for each other, and each person donated something to the Christmas dinner. Kate had six potatoes left from the supply her father had sent to her, and even if they were frozen they were a wonderful treat. Christmas Day began with a church service in which the Reverend John Pringle favoured his congregation with one of his most eloquent sermons. He assured them of Almighty God's protection and exhorted them to help each other, obeying the golden rule of brotherly love. If they would follow that basic rule, he said, they would live through the winter in Atlin. The meal that followed Reverend Pringle's sermon seemed to be blessed indeed, for that Christmas Day feast turned into one of the finest meals any of them could ever remember. In later years, Pringle referred to that winter in Atlin as one of the most difficult of his career.

"Had it not been for the sense of community and camaraderie in Atlin during the winter of 1898, few would have survived," he said. "The fierce determination from all brought the small group through the most difficult of winters under desperate conditions."

There was no calm or tranquillity when the spring of 1899 finally came. Miners and prospectors suffering from scurvy, frost bite and cabin fever all tumbled from their cabins and crude hovels to stretch in the warm spring sun and look again towards the Klondike. Freed from the torments of winter, they soon forgot their hardships as they rushed to the creek beds looking for the gold that had brought them to this godforsaken land. The sun melted the diggings from the previous fall, and more and more of the elusive wealth exposed itself to the waiting world. Turmoil became hysteria. In Atlin, Kate and her friends packed up and hit the trail with the first signs of spring. From Atlin, their route went across Atlin Lake to Taku, up Taku Arm and over to Nares Lake. From Nares Lake, the travellers made for Caribou Crossing (later called Carcross), where they finally rejoined a semblance of civilization. The White Pass and Yukon Railway had already reached Caribou Crossing, and with the spring thaw the crews continued cutting the trail through the woods between Caribou Crossing and Whitehorse. The seasoned travellers of the Teslin Trail considered this rough cut through the woods a brisk walk.

Of the thousands of stampeders who had chosen the All Canadian Route to the Klondike gold fields, only a few hundred pressed on to the Yukon. The Yukon Field Force had prepared the way for those fortunate enough to make it to Teslin City, over the lake system and down the Yukon River by raft. A few made it to Atlin from Glenora, while many more were stranded at various points along the trails. When the spring rains melted the ice in the rivers, the men of the north filled the waterways, and both flowed into the Yukon with the spring floods of 1899. Kate walked the miles to her next destination with a bounce in her step. All along the route she met men and women who had survived the winter and could now appreciate the beauty of the Yukon. Finally, four miles down the Yukon River from the Whitehorse Rapids, Kate arrived at Whitehorse. Still a tent town, Whitehorse had nevertheless become a hustling, bustling trading centre for travellers from every corner of the globe coming and going along the golden route to Dawson. As soon as she got her bearings, Kate pitched her tent and posted her sign, "Kate's Café — Open For Business." She no sooner had her sign up and a pot of coffee boiling when her first customer, Dominic Burns, stopped in.

"Well, you finally made it, eh, Kate," he teased. "Sure am proud to see you here, but, well, hell, you should change your sign."

Kate looked at her friend in puzzlement. "What do you mean,

Dominic? Don't you like the sign? Is there something wrong with it?"

"Well, no, but now that you've made it to the Klondike, why don't you call it 'Klondike Kate's Café'?"

Kate didn't know whether to take him seriously or not, so she laughed at his proposition, but the idea appealed to her customers. The word spread, and before long her new business was "Klondike Kate's Café" even if she didn't change the sign out front.

Kate worked night and day to keep up with the trade that came to her little café. During July and August, she had to hire a woman to help her, and both kept up a frantic pace from early morning until late in the evening. Kate continued to take in laundry, and served as a nurse whenever she was needed, too. She never charged for her nursing work, and accepted money only when it was offered by a patient who she knew could afford to pay. It was against her way to charge for helping someone in a bad fix.

The days were never long enough, even in the land of the midnight sun, and Kate worked furiously in the knowledge that this was her one opportunity to make her stake. She invested readily in miners' claims and was quick to grubstake some she knew well. She also had her own Free Miner's License and enjoyed a fair bit of success in some of the mines near Whitehorse. She believed that she would profit most if she kept working at what she knew best and put her money to work by investing it in men and mines that she felt were going to make it. Her prosperity put the idea of going on to Dawson further and further from her mind.

The completion of the White Pass and Yukon Railway was a historic event for the whole Yukon, but Whitehorse reacted by picking itself up and moving across the river to the junction. On July 30, 1900, when the first train arrived in Whitehorse from the other terminal in Skagway, Alaska, the town began to plant permanent roots. Kate decided that she would never again spend a winter in a tent. Perhaps an urge to mix the precious package of Johnville soil in the bottom of her leather bag with the earth of a new home prompted her to hire two men to build her a frame

Ceremony of driving the last spike at Whitehorse, June 8, 1900.

(NAC, ©Hudson's Bay Company)

house. Her "great big home," as she called it, was one of the first wooden structures in the new town of Whitehorse. On a lot behind the one purchased by the Bank of Commerce, Kate's house was not only central to the business community but in a spot where her café could prosper.

As the first snowflakes of 1900 fluttered over the town of Whitehorse, Kate could sigh with relief as she put a log in her new stove. For the first time in almost two years, she felt the security of sound walls, a solid floor and real curtains, all of which were to be her protection against the long winter ahead. Her one room cabin, only 12' by 16', was not much larger that her tent, but it rested on blocks above the permafrost. Safe and secure, she confided to her friends that it was a palace for a woman who had spent the last two winters in a tent. Her home and business remained one for a short time, but before long the restaurant outgrew the little house. When Norman Macaulay offered her a place in his new hotel, she was delighted to move her business there.

Macauley had arrived in the Whitehorse area a couple of years earlier. Realizing that his fortune lay not in the creek beds, but in the service of those who were looking for gold, he had

Kate's first home, Whitehorse, 1900. (Walter Ryan)

constructed a wooden tram line along the bank of the Yukon River to bypass Miles Canyon and the vicious Whitehorse Rapids. Because few of the gold seekers were expert boatmen, and because the rapids were so dangerous, Macauley could charge $25 a load to transport goods and passengers overland around the dangers of the river. The White Pass and Yukon Railway soon made Macauley's tram obsolete, but he had already raked in enough money to establish himself in business and build a splendid hotel. The Whitehorse *Star* declared the Whitehorse Hotel one of the most modern in the Yukon, a first-class establishment in every respect. It boasted meeting rooms, lounges, a games room and that utmost luxury, private baths and indoor conveniences — though not the kind that used running water. The restaurant was under the proprietorship of Miss Kate Ryan.

The town spread as transients came and went along the route to Dawson. Some stayed just for the summer months, while others decided to make Whitehorse their permanent home. John Pringle remained in Atlin for the time being, but he often visited the town. Frank Burd set up the Whitehorse *Tribune*, a short-lived newspaper financed by Vancouver interests. Although Frank did not stay long, he and Kate became friends, and their friendship continued for many years. Philip Primrose now commanded the Whitehorse North West Mounted Police detachment. Henry Corcoran, Kate's friend from Johnville, had made the long trek to the Yukon to make his fortune before returning home to marry the girl of his dreams. Whitehorse also acquired a permanent priest, Father Jean LeFebvre, who came as a missionary. His arrival was a great consolation to Kate, because once again she could worship regularly in her own faith. Now that they had a priest, she and a few members of the small parish started a building fund and worked feverishly to raise enough money to construct a church. They sent letters requesting donations to New Brunswick and the United States, to friends and relatives everywhere. Soon Whitehorse Catholics realized their dreams; they had built themselves a modest church.

The North West Mounted Police established their first detachment at Whitehorse in 1898, first under the supervision of Francis Richard, who maintained order with the help of a sergeant and three constables. The surge of struggling humanity into the Yukon and the rapid transition from wilderness to wealth brought overwhelming problems. The burden of control fell on the shoulders of the North West Mounted Police, and only thanks to their diligence, integrity and discipline did the Yukon survive the first chaotic years. They ruled the territory with an iron hand, not only minimizing crime and suffering, but also — unknown to many — preventing a revolution.

Everyone in Whitehorse understood the very definite class distinctions in the town. On the one side were the government representatives, bankers, business people, miners and working men, and on the other side were the gamblers, prostitutes and other disreputables. On the lowest rungs of the social ladder, the soubrettes and their assistants installed themselves across the railway tracks from their betters in a community aptly called Lousetown. The line between the two classes was firmly drawn. The people of the saloons came mainly from the American Midwest, following the gold rushes from one strike to another. For the most part they were professional hucksters with a code of ethics summed up by one of their female representatives: "Make as much money as possible and get out quick — preferably ahead of the law." One young woman apparently attempting to abide by this golden rule was Kitty Rockwell. According to her own report, in 1899 she reached the end of the White Pass and Yukon Railway line at Bennett. For two months, she sang and danced in a saloon there to replenish her pocketbook, and then she pressed onward toward the Klondike. By this time, so many inexperienced men had been killed trying to shoot the Whitehorse Rapids that the North West Mounted Police forbade anyone to attempt the trip except under supervision, and they made women walk the five miles around the rapids instead of braving them with the men. Kitty would have none of this. Dressed as a boy, she waited until a boat was about to cast off, and then darted from the crowd and leapt aboard the boat too late for the police constable to catch her. Once in Whitehorse, she plied her trade until she received an offer to join the Savoy theatrical troupe rehearsing in Victoria to perform in Dawson the next spring. Having cut a sufficient swath in Whitehorse, Kitty retraced her journey instead of continuing to Dawson alone.

While excitement and hoopla took over Dawson, 380 miles away, Whitehorse seemed to be overlooked by the more rambunctious criminals. Instead of leading a flamboyant life of dance-halls and gambling dens, Whitehorse continued the steady growth of a pioneer settlement, with church and town hall creating a permanent, stable society. Dawson, however, remained wide open during 1899 and 1900, with dance-hall girls and saloons operating freely. When the Yukon Field Force arrived in Dawson, it pressed some order upon the so-far uncontrolled town. The Queen's army also brought government officials and a Victorian social attitude that demanded enforcement of the laws of Canada.

A leader in this challenge to the north was Henry Woodside. Henry had made the journey to Dawson from Glenora with the army and became editor of the Dawson *Sun*. In its pages he began his own crusade to shut down the saloons, and his assistant in this missionary work was none other than the Reverend John Pringle. They instigated a bombardment of letters and telegrams asking their representatives in Ottawa to curtail the vice and disorder rampant in Dawson and, to a lesser extent, Whitehorse. While the battle raged between the two social

Henry Woodside, 1901. (HJW/NAC)

groups, the North West Mounted Police felt a great deal of pressure to stop the gambling and the blatant solicitation by the ladies of the night.

Events in another part of Canada also had a direct effect on the dance hall queens of the north. In what would become Alberta, a group of the first suffragettes, organized under the banner of the Women's Christian Temperance Union, lobbied the Canadian Government to improve the treatment of women prisoners. In Feb-ruary 1900, parliament passed a law that a "woman special" would be hired to assist any member of the North West Mounted Police with a woman prisoner. On February 5, 1900, Kate Ryan became the first "woman special," attached to the North West Mounted Police, Whitehorse, Yukon detachment.

Hot Times in Whitehorse

Kate felt secure in her snug new home. Confident of financial success from her mining investments, she still continued to supervise and maintain the restaurant in the Whitehorse Hotel. She could also add the $2 a day she received as a North West Mounted Police Constable Special to her growing bank account. Her part-time job as matron at the jail began as incidental work, but soon it became a full-time headache for both Kate and the police. As matron, Kate was on call to attend any women the police jailed. Her own physical appearance demanded respect, and the air of authority with which she carried herself made her an imposing figure. The women with whom she had to work gave her little difficulty. Sentences for the women who got into trouble with the law were usually minor, and incarceration meant an overnight stay in jail, or, at most, just long enough to have a "silent partner" (a business man who was looking after his investment) pay a fine. Kate was well aware that she could do nothing to change the social or moral values of the women who were working the saloons of Whitehorse, so she followed the law to the letter and made no judgements.

While ordinary citizens went about their daily lives, Major Zachary T. Woods received a telegram from his superiors in Ottawa declaring that all dance-halls and gambling casinos were to be closed as of June 1, 1900. This law represented a victory for the citizens who had lobbied against these dens of iniquity, and Henry Woodside and Reverend John Pringle were elated. The owners of the dance-halls and saloons realized their days were numbered. Grateful that they still had time to improve their investments in the huge stocks of liquor and cigars they had stockpiled, they reduced their prices and threw open their doors for a grand party. When the news reached the streets of Dawson, the town "was painted a mild vermilion, the faro banks were played as heavily as in the good old days, the girls were in the streets in squads dressed in their best bibs and tuckers." The extension to June 1 gave the saloon-keepers time to "clean up,

Kate in Whitehorse. (KMK)

before the town closed and transformed into a graveyard." In contrast, Whitehorse celebrated St. Patrick's Day with the town decorated in green ribbons and homemade Irish flags. Father LeFebvre celebrated a High Mass, which was followed by a concert of Irish music and poetry. Mrs. Minnie Tache played the organ, and the new North West Mounted Police Inspector, Fitz Horrigan, won the hearts of the ladies as he sang a rendition of "Danny Boy." Other musicians and elocutionists added their talents to the concert. The evening was extended to include a farewell party for the very popular Major Phillip Primrose, who had been promoted and transferred to Dawson.

Primrose's promotion and transfer did not pique curiosity in Whitehorse; it was understood that he was being sent to enforce the closure of the saloons and gambling houses. But there was a hidden reason for his quick departure. Certainly when he arrived in Dawson he began to enforce the new laws, closing the gambling halls and turning Dawson into the anticipated graveyard. The saloons emptied as quickly as they had filled, the music from the player pianos ceased, and cobwebs and dust collected on the once-polished bars as the mountains silently watched events unfold. On Christmas Eve, 1900, the Arctic wind blew with all its fury on the city of Dawson. In the winter darkness, miners dreamed of warm summer days, creek-beds overflowing their banks and sluice boxes filled with rock speckled with brilliant yellow gold. But while the miners dreamed one dream,

North West Mounted Police detachment at Whitehorse with Fitz Horrigan (far left) and Phillip Primrose (third from left, centre row).

(NAC)

other more practical men had different visions. The gold of which they dreamed had already been unearthed and now lay in strong-boxes in Dawson and Whitehorse. These realists resented the authority imposed upon them by the same ill-informed government two thousand miles away that had closed the saloons and turned Dawson into a veritable ghost town. The northern prospectors deeply despised this foreign government and felt no allegiance toward it. During the long dark hours, these men had little to think about except the riches that were so near, and they were overcome with greed. While the lights of Dawson blazed in celebration of Christmas, deep in its bowels a handful of men met on December 26 to plan a revolution.

Unaware of the boiling unrest in Dawson, Kate Ryan and her friends also held a meeting of a completely different nature. The first official gathering of the North Star Athletic Club was held on January 3. The new members elected their first slate of officers and outlined their objectives. Businessman Bob Lowe was elected the first president, with Kate, Minnie Taylor and George Pringle as the first directors and the Reverend John Wright as the club padre. The objectives of the group were, first, to act as a meeting place for community social and sporting events, and second, to use the proceeds of their events to assist in the growth of their town. Their first big project would be a financial drive to establish their desperately needed hospital. Whitehorse had grown by leaps and bounds from its beginnings as a tent city, and now it had begun to take the shape of a modern town. It included a fire hall, a post office, a train station, a school and five flourishing hotels. The town's weekly newspaper, the Whitehorse *Star*, carried advertisements for Fred McLennan's hardware store, which offered a complete line of hockey skates for young and old alike. Dominic Burns, ever the entrepreneur, now owned butcher shops in Bennett, Atlin, Whitehorse, Pine City and Dawson. The White Pass and Yukon Railway operated on a regular schedule, and by all modern standards, Whitehorse was a town on the way up. Small gold strikes were still being reported in the outlying districts, but the great rush of '98 had begun to subside as large mining companies and investors came in and took over the big operations.

Kate enjoyed a busy schedule, employing two women in the restaurant and working part-time as prison matron. She made regular trips to view her mining investments, and kept her Free Miner's Licence, which allowed her to pan for gold herself or invest in any operations that seemed promising. An informal club gathered every morning at Kate's restaurant in the Whitehorse Hotel to drink coffee and exchange gossip. Major A.E. Snyder, Inspector Primrose's replacement and Fitz Horrigan, his assistant, were both regulars at these coffee meetings. Fitz was a favourite with the public because of his jovial good humour and his participation in the Athletic Club functions. Whitehorse merchants, all of whom were members of the Athletic Club, belonged to the coffee group, as did the local prospectors, who came in to find out the current gold prices as well as to catch up on the latest gossip. Travelling salesmen would join when they came to town, contributing the valuable information they brought in from outside. In a community the size of Whitehorse, it was impossible to keep secrets, and all rumours and reports were dissected at the morning round table discussions.

The majority of the population supported the closure of the saloons, but those who had made fortunes in the casinos were

Bob Lowe (left) and Kate (right) with friends in Whitehorse. (KMK)

outraged at the stupidity of the act. The American population of the Yukon that had flooded in at the first sound of the word "gold" felt that when the Alaskan boundary dispute was settled the whole Yukon would be turned over to the United States. Rumours of unrest grew in frequency and velocity and became one of the main topics of discussion at the Whitehorse morning coffee meetings as well as throughout the territory. For some unstated reason, Major Snyder kept his entire detachment of 63 men on constant alert.

Fred Clark, who supervised a crew of men out on the Big Salmon, had begun the habit of joining the morning group. He came to town on the pretext of buying supplies for the camp, but the locals treated him as an outsider and gave him a wide berth. When Bob Lowe remarked that he would not trust Clark,

Kate told of her first encounter with the man. She had meet him and his partner, Ozzie Frith, in Atlin on the way in. Clark considered himself smarter than everyone else and didn't mind saying so. He and Ozzie managed to avoid the customs at Atlin and bragged about outsmarting the yellow-legs. It wasn't long before Constable Alex Menzies caught up with the would-be smugglers and made them pay up. Everyone in Atlin thought it was a great joke, but Clark had raised Cain with every official he could corner. He complained that because he was an American citizen he wasn't obliged to pay any goddamn Canadian taxes. Everyone else ignored his wrath, silently glad that he got what was coming to him. Clark continued to frequent the Whitehorse Hotel, and he asked a lot of questions. Bob told Kate that he found him more offensive and louder than usual, and they wondered what he was up to this time. On one occasion, Kate noticed that when Fitz came into the dining room, Clark disappeared. His sudden departure was so evident that she asked Fitz what he had on the notorious smuggler that had sent him scurrying. Fitz laughed but did concede that Clark and his cronies were up to no good, and asked her to keep a sharp eye on his comings and goings. A certain group of men continually gave the customs and other government officials a difficult time, their aim apparently to pay absolutely no royalties or duties imposed by the Canadian government. Rumours of a revolt persisted in Whitehorse, and Snyder telegraphed to Primrose that he was worried about what might take place. He cautioned Primrose that although the unrest seemed to be confined to the American miners, they had a lot of sympathy from the other miners who all felt the royalties were unfair and too high. The Americans persevered in their belief that the Yukon belonged to the United States, never for a moment considering the earth in which they were digging to be Canadian soil.

The steamers that flooded into the Yukon in the spring of 1901 were filled as usual with salesmen, carpet-baggers, tradesmen and adventurers. They flowed into Whitehorse with much less effort than those who had struggled into the settlement in previous years, but the opening of the waterways always brought an influx of new faces and an upsurge in business. Outside investors believed strongly in the resources of the Yukon and poured millions of dollars into the mines and the economy. Wages were at an all time high, and anyone willing to work hard could make excellent money in the short summer season. One of the new faces arriving in Whitehorse that spring belonged to an American of German descent named Herman Grehl. He was only in town a few days when he set up a ferry service across the Yukon River just above Whitehorse. This new convenience was an original idea as well as a practical one, and the fledgling businessman soon made the acquaintance of most of the local inhabitants. The North Star Athletic Club decided to take advantage of the new service and organized their first picnic at Norman Macauley's old terminal across the river. The plan was so popular that on the appointed Sunday afternoon, Grehl was overwhelmed with the members and their guests who joined in the excursion to cross the river for a Sunday outing. Grehl was a powerful man with broad shoulders. Although his speech was thick and gruff, he was friendly, and on first encounter he charmed the ladies with his European flair and polished manners. Bob Lowe and Kate had organized the day's events. They were delighted at the success and somewhat surprised when both Major Snyder and Fitz Horrigan attended the affair with their companions.

On June 24, a few weeks after the picnic, an incident in Skagway, Alaska, caused grave concern at Whitehorse North West Mounted Police headquarters. In accordance with international law, Edward S. Busby, the Canadian customs representative in charge of the Skagway office, was flying the Union Jack over the customs building. In the early afternoon, a rowdy, boisterous crowd of men gathered, led by Andrew Miller, Skagway's most important lawyer. Without provocation from Busby or any of his employees, the men cut down the Canadian flag, to the tune of wild cheers and shouts from the mob. Busby rushed out to raise the flag again, but he found himself surrounded by a group of very hostile men. They ordered him to raise the American flag above the Canadian flag, and when he refused, he found himself in a delicate predicament. After much shouted abuse and intimidation, Busby agreed to notify his superiors in Ottawa, and until he received further orders, no flag at all would be raised. When the crowd finally cooled down, Busby wired Major Snyder in Whitehorse for advice and help. To alleviate the pressure, Snyder ordered Busby back to the Canadian boundary line.

This flag incident sparked all the hidden tensions between the opposing parties in the boundary dispute. Canadian and American newspapers began a verbal battle, each slandering the opposing government. The notorious Skagway papers took particular delight in discrediting the North West Mounted Police, portraying the men as the evil tools of an unjust government. The underlying cause, of course, was the economic and physical battle for the possession of the wealth of the north. Prime Minister Wilfrid Laurier monitored the situation, growing more and more concerned about the unfolding events. He was determined to keep the territory that rightfully belonged to Canada, but, even before the gold rush, he had said, "The most important issue just now, as affecting the relations and friendly feeling between Canada and the United States, is the Alaska Boundary question. The situation is full of danger and all that is required to precipitate a disgraceful conflict is the discovery of gold in the disputed territory." Under the surface of that "friendly feeling" was a struggle that, with a little help from the Mother Country, Canada was about to lose. Even though the public took the flag incident rather lightly, Laurier ordered Primrose in Dawson and Snyder in Whitehorse to purchase new Lee-Enfield rifles and man the two Maxim guns at Whitehorse and the one in Dawson. The public joked that the North West Mounted Police were going to war.

As the summer wore on, Kate could see that Snyder and Horrigan were worried, and that they kept a constant watch on the ferryman, Grehl. Snyder dropped remarks to Kate as she went about her matron's duties, and he asked her to report any unusual happenings. He warned her to be cautious in her dealings with the German. Grehl himself began to frequent the hotels, and soon he and Fred Clark set up a business partnership. They established their Alaskan-Yukon Forwarding Company in an office behind the Pioneer Hotel. In August, Clark left for Skagway, telling everyone in town that he had been promoted and that he was going to set up the main office. Shortly afterwards, Grehl went to Dawson to start another branch. Both men flashed a lot of money around, but no one ever saw either of them actually doing any business.

Few in Whitehorse knew that the North West Mounted Police had engaged the Pinkerton Detective Agency from the United States to investigate the backgrounds of the two men. Pinkerton's soon confirmed their worst suspicions: the two were involved in a dangerous plot to overthrow the North West Mounted Police and seize the Yukon Territory. Armed with this information, the Police took quick action. Primrose in Dawson and Snyder in Whitehorse called in their senior staff and outlined the situation. On September 20, Inspector Cortland Starnes sent his report to the commanding officer.

> Sir: I have the honour to report that on Tuesday evening a man named H. Grehl had told another man named Max Heilberger that he knew of a conspiracy that was going to take place against the government. This man was located in the Pioneer Saloon and McGuire heard the conversation. This conversation was to the effect that Grehl belonged to a secret organization that intended to take possession of the Yukon Territory. Their plans were to rush Whitehorse and take the smaller detachments along the river and then, as there were only about 200 men in the police force, it would be an easy matter to take the police barracks at Dawson . . . They expect men to assist them from Circle City and Eagle City. The first movement on their part is to cut the telegraph wires . . . Grehl is being watched.

Obviously the Alaskan-Yukon Forwarding Company was nothing but a front for the conspiracy, and Fred Clark and Herman Grehl were organizing a rebellion. Superintendent Zachary T. Wood wired to ask the Skagway authorities to arrest Fred Clark when he arrived there. The same day, he sent Philip Primrose from Dawson to Skagway to collect information and papers that, they had learned, were in the company safe in Skagway. Primrose made a hasty trip to Whitehorse, where he and Snyder discussed the information they had gathered about the conspiracy. They agreed to be on the alert and to act quickly and secretly.

The reputation earned by the town of Skagway during the early days of the Gold Rush was well deserved, and many cutthroats and hooligans still occupied the border town. The settlement operated according to its own set of laws, and the unsuspecting Primrose walked right into a hornet's nest. The business community of Skagway was fed up with losing the revenue diverted by Canadian laws into Canadian hands. They were angry over the Alaskan boundary dispute, and resented the interference and strong-arm tactics of the North West Mounted Police. In fact, they saw the Police as the main cause of their problems, and had no intention of giving Phillip Primrose any assistance. News of Primrose's arrival spread like wildfire, and his enemies knew that at long last they would have revenge on the hated "yellow-legs." Within a couple of hours, Primrose had been sidetracked and thrown in the Skagway jail, charged with drunkenness, insulting the American flag and disorderly conduct. The Skagway *News* delighted in reporting of Primrose's misfortune. "Primrose In Disgrace, Rotten Police," the headline screamed, and the subhead was even worse: "Bad Brand of Hooch must have been opened in the City last night." The story continued:

> Either the weather or a remarkable hilarious brand of liquor has had a marked effect on several people in Skagway yesterday. In the Commissioner's court, Inspector Primrose of the North West Police Force paid into the coffers of the United States Government. The gentleman was accompanied by his friend Count Alexander Carbonneau "Wish s'had picture of my fren's," said the culprit, looking at the curious crowd that had collected. In answer the Count pointed to a suggestive sign, some wag had placed on the blackboard which read "No Tick" . . . Inspector Primrose pleaded guilty and the court assessed a fine of $10 and costs.

The Skagway paper went to great lengths to exaggerate Primrose's "night on the town," the same town that had become world famous for desperados and thugs. With the help of a few cool heads, Primrose was finally bailed out of jail, but not before he had been harassed and publicly ridiculed. Furious, Primrose boarded the White Pass and Yukon train for Whitehorse. Rumours worse than the actual events preceded him. Although few believed the stories, Primrose was disgraced. His Whitehorse friends helped him, but he heard the odd snicker from the sidelines all the same.

Emblem of the
Order of the Midnight Sun.
(San Francisco *Call*, Nov. 17, 1901)

Primrose did not get the evidence he had been sent for, but he had enough information to assure his superiors that Skagway was a hotbed of discontent and that the business community and the public officials supported the planned insurrection. Police headquarters at Whitehorse and Dawson buzzed with activity, everyone was sworn to secrecy, and Kate moved in and out of her work asking few questions. Coded messages flooded the telegraph wires. "Snyder reports discovered whereabouts in Skagway papers relating to conspiracy to seize territory. United States refuses to secure unless Snyder makes affidavit as to conspirators. This of course he cannot do. Am satisfied such conspiracies exist. Signed Z.T. Wood." A coded message to Major A.B. Perry, in Regina, read, "Private cipher. Otho implication rhapsodical restoring intrenchment corroborate shunted pretermission custom." Translated, this meant, "Whitehorse reports, reliable information, conspiracy seize Porcupine Country." The incredulous Major Perry immediately telegraphed his superior to inform the Prime Minister.

Similar coded messages flew back and forth between Alaska

and Washington. The American officials were embarrassed and worried. It had been strongly implied that American citizens had funded the conspiracy, and since no one would identify these citizens, speculation mounted. The Pinkerton Agency, still working for the Canadian government, discovered that Grehl, a grocer from Butte, Montana, had very strong financial backing from some unknown source. Not wanting to be implicated, Washington ordered Skagway officials to support the Canadians' requests for assistance. Reluctantly, they agreed to do so. For his part, Laurier sent his own urgent telegram: "Do nothing that will create an international incident."

Canadian and American officials came together at a hastily-organized meeting in Skagway. This meeting was the best-kept secret of the decade, reported only in a short press release which mentioned a "Junta" and gave assurance that American authorities would repress the filibustering outfit at Skagway. But, in their caution to repress damaging evidence, the officials forgot about the revolutionaries themselves. As the officials met in Skagway, Fred Clark beat a hasty retreat by steamer to Seattle. Forewarned of his arrival, a reporter from the Seattle *Daily Times* met Clark at the dock and paid him a very handsome price for the documents so desperately sought by Inspector Primrose.

The reporter could scarcely believe his good fortune, for the information Clark sold him was far more incriminating than he had ever imagined. The package of documents included the complete official papers of an organization known as the Order of the Midnight Sun. An advisory board elected at the Order's first meeting, held on December 26, 1900, wrote and distributed a manifesto containing 19 points of dispute with the Canadian government. The complaints included everything from defective mining laws and corrupt officials to dissatisfaction with the way the boundary dispute was being handled to grievances about the strict laws against gambling, liquor and prostitution. The Order's hair-raising oath included a promise that members would never reveal the organization's secrets which members swore to under penalty of death and signed in blood. Other papers showed that the Order's leaders intended actually to kill any members who broke the code of secrecy. Fred Clark's portfolio contained the official seals and emblems, oaths signed by the members and

Seal of the
Order of the Midnight Sun.
(San Francisco *Call*, Nov. 17, 1901)

damaging correspondence, and he gratefully turned all this over to the reporter in return for the cash he needed to finance his escape.

Clark's papers outlined the whole plan for the seizure of the Yukon, complete with maps, orders and directions to secret caches of guns and supplies. It would go into effect at freeze-up, because, the conspirators thought, winter would give them six months' immunity from intervention. At a prearranged signal, the telegraph lines would be cut at twelve points simultaneously, and at that moment the revolution would begin. The North West Mounted Police posts at Whitehorse and Dawson would be taken first, by members of the Order of the Midnight Sun living in each town. Then the leaders would establish the "Klondike Free State." The founders and the advisory board would form the government until a "democratic" election could be held; alternatively, help would arrive from the United States. The revolutionaries were convinced that the world would consider them heroes, and believed without question that the United States government supported their efforts. The Seattle *Daily Times* published a complete report, illustrated with photographs, emblems and an outline of the manifesto, on the front page. The exclusive interview with Fred Clark concluded, "But the leaders of the conspiracy lacked the requisite nerve. Someone 'leaked' and the Order of the Midnight Sun, it is believed, will disappear as quietly and completely as the snow banks on the reaches of the Upper Yukon with the first rays of the sun in May."

While the citizens of Seattle enjoyed their news stories, Inspector Primrose and Major Snyder still had to deal with the men in their midst awaiting the signal to start the revolution. Under the Prime Minister's command not to start an international incident, Primrose and Snyder started their counter-espionage. Two stories that surfaced a short time before freeze-up seemed to have connections to the cautious men of the force. In the haze of a late fall night, a dirty and haggard prospector lurched his way up the main street of Dawson and into the Monte Carlo Saloon. Bearded and unkempt, he resembled hundreds of other down-on-their-luck men in town. At the bar, he shouted for attention, threw down a good-sized poke of gold, and ordered drinks all round. The music stopped and gamblers and drinkers gathered around and plied him with questions. At first, he remained evasive, baiting his audience with his shy manner and his refusal to tell them where he had made the biggest strike in the Klondike. The more he drank, the more garrulous he became. The drinking continued, until well into the night, when he opened up with a tale of this new strike, of how he had found his fortune and how wealth beyond the dreams of avarice waited there for his return. The audience cheered. The celebration went on and on. Finally, the prospector relented. He divulged the name and location of his secret creek, just inside the Alaska border. The Monte Carlo cleared as if by magic. The leaders of the rebellion, which was to begin in the next few days, struggled in vain to keep their men in line. Most poured from the town towards the new strike in Alaska. It was said that the stranger never did return to Alaska himself but made his way around behind the saloon to sneak into the back of Inspector Primrose's cabin. He was never seen again.

In Whitehorse, Snyder found out that Grehl had developed a double-cross of his own. He intended to use the revolution to rob the bank. He had no allegiance to any country, much less to the Order of the Midnight Sun. On his customary walk to Kate's Café for his morning coffee, Snyder saw the genial Grehl approaching. Grehl greeted Snyder cheerfully, as usual. With a smile, Snyder looked him straight in the eye and remarked, "A hell of a job, this bank hold-up scheme, eh?"

The German stuttered and stammered. "What's that? A bank hold-up? What do you mean?"

"Oh, you know all about the Order of the Midnight Sun, don't you?" Snyder persisted.

Grehl feigned ignorance. "The Midnight Sun? Certainly, right above heads."

"Not that midnight sun," Snyder patiently explained, "the Order of the Midnight Sun — the new organization. It's an outfit of damned fools who think they can rob the banks at Dawson and Whitehorse."

"Do you know about it?" blurted Grehl, not realizing how deeply he implicated himself.

"Oh, yes, all about it," Snyder replied.

"What are you going to do?" asked the nervous Grehl.

"That's up to me. But we'll give them all a merry time."

Before Grehl could close his mouth, Snyder turned and went into the Cafe for his morning coffee. As he sat stirring his third cup, one of his constables hurried in to report that two men had been seen hiking out of town on the railway ties, travelling light and fast. Snyder laid his change on the counter, winked at Kate and strolled over to headquarters. He sent the constable to wire a message to the outpost at Caribou Crossing telling his men to watch for two men on foot and ordering them to let the men pass without questioning them. Some time later, a return telegram reported that the two men had just crossed the Canadian-American border. For all Snyder cared, the two could walk to the equator. That evening, a small group of friends gathered at Kate's house for a private celebration. Major Snyder, Fitz Horrigan, Bob Lowe and a few others toasted the Queen, the Prime Minister and in particular the overthrow of a rebellion no one else realized was imminent. Most of all, they toasted the beginning of a prosperous new era for the Yukon.

Kate in uniform as a "Constable Special" with "H" Division of the North West Mounted Police, Whitehorse. (KMK)

Sergeant Kate and Klondike Kate

On *December 2, 1901,* the Whitehorse *Star* published a news report that summed up the rebellion as far as the people were concerned. "At present, in spite of the statement 'the scare is over,' maxim guns command the highways of Whitehorse and the police are doing double duty." The aura of the Order of the Midnight Sun faded as quickly as it had illuminated the northern sky. With guns mounted and pointed at the unknown enemy, the citizens of Whitehorse went about their business as usual, without thinking of war or putting locks on their doors.

Content that Fred Clark and the ferryman Grehl had fled to some southern country, Kate returned to the ordinary events of her life. The year 1901 had been a financial success for her; she had made gains from her shares in a copper mine, and her investment in a small gold mine also paid good dividends. Calculating her year's receipts, she realized that by all standards she had achieved financial security for the first time in her life. For the last year, every letter from her mother had asked the same question: when was she coming home? With her steady investment income and a good bank account behind her, Kate decided she could finally go home. She made her reservations to leave Whitehorse and arrive in Johnville in time for Christmas.

The women working in the restaurant agreed to take over for the winter months. That settled, she asked Major Snyder for a leave of absence from her prison matron's job. Snyder granted her leave only on condition that she promise him firmly to return.

"Oh, sure'n you don't think for a minute that I would not come back to Whitehorse?" Kate teased him.

"Well, Miss Kate, I can tell you we can't run this country without you, so you have to come back," Snyder replied.

Kate flushed at Snyder's flattery and assured him she would

never dream of failing to return to her home in the north. But as they both knew, many more had left the north with promises to return, only to change their minds once they reached the outside.

Kate boarded a White Pass and Yukon Railway coach filled with excited passengers elated to be finally on their way outside for the winter. Kate was overwhelmed with anticipation. She was not only heading outside but was going home for the first time in seven years. The train began its slow way along the tracks to the Canadian-United States border. Suddenly she was filled with sadness. As she watched the magnificent scenery pass the window of the train, her memory filled with the images of her own epic struggle to reach the Yukon. Seated in the luxurious comfort of the dark red plush seat, she called up visions of the pack trains, dog sleds, camp fires and blizzards that had marked her journey into the north. The settlements of Glenora, Teslin City and Atlin seemed a long way off now, as if she had dreamed them all. Through the mountains the train rumbled on to Skagway. Her trip outside had taken seven hours; her expedition in had taken over a year. The luxury steamer *Islander* waited at the dock for the holiday passengers bound for Vancouver, Victoria, Seattle and all points south.

Kate's first destination was a long-overdue visit with Mary and Patrick Haley in Seattle, complete with a much-anticipated shopping spree. Kate had written to her cousin to be prepared: she was going to buy a whole new wardrobe — Kate Ryan would go home in style. After a week in Seattle, she boarded the train for her transcontinental journey. During her trip across the United States, travellers who found out about her Yukon experience surprised her with their kindness and curiosity. She was amazed at the stories they related to her about the Yukon and the legend that, unknown to Kate, had evolved in the outside world around the name "Klondike Kate." The miles fell behind as the train crossed state after state, until at last Kate crossed the border back into Canada. The train began to wind its way up the St. John River Valley, and familiar scenes and villages sped past the windows. The December darkness descended upon the moving train as the conductor called the stopping places: "Woodstock, Hartland, Stickney, Florenceville, Bristol." With each stop, Kate's excitement rose. Finally the conductor made a call especially for her: "Next stop, Bath and Johnville." Kate nervously gathered her parcels and clutched her well-worn black bag for security. The conductor smiled with pride as he came along the aisle to assist his famous passenger. Her new dress rustled beneath the folds of her full-length sable coat, and she adjusted her hat, trying to gather her composure. The train screeched to a halt and, with the poise of the true lady that she was, Kate Ryan descended the cold steel steps of the hissing train. Through the train's billowing vapours the haloed lights of the station added their festive spirit to the lanterns of the cheering group waiting to greet their home-town heroine.

Kate was overcome by the exuberant welcome. She received attention and admiration everywhere she went. Never in her wildest dreams had she imagined how widespread and important the stories of the Yukon had become on the outside. The glamour of the gold rush obsessed many people, and they longed to hear stories about it from the lips of one who had herself become a legend. At times she had to scoff at the exaggerations making the rounds, yet she had to admit that there was a lot of truth in some of the stories of the Yukon. She was such a celebrity in her own little community that the local newspaper sent a reporter up to her family's farm for an exclusive interview. But she was much more concerned with being home with her mother and family. Christmas was always her favourite time of the year, and it was exciting to share in the Johnville festivities and see the changes among her friends and relatives. Midnight Mass at St. John the Evangelist was a night of reminiscence. So little had changed, yet so much. Smells, sights and sounds remained the same — balsam tinged with incense, evergreen boughs trimmed with ribbons, candles casting their shimmering shadows. The church filled with familiar faces — friendly faces she recognized from her younger days, families now clutching the tiny hands of children Kate recognized as copies of their parents. Smiles and nods greeted her when she took her place in the Ryan pew as if it had been just last Sunday that she left. Basking in the warmth of the familiar sights, Kate suddenly caught her breath as Simon Gallagher entered the church escorting his recent bride to the Gallagher pew. Kate had prepared herself for the inevitable encounter, but still a shiver ran up her spine. As they passed in front of her, she gave no sign of uneasiness, but nodded politely as Simon recognized her. The congregation rose with the entrance of the priest on the altar. "*Introibo ad altare Dei,*" he chanted, as Kate was once more united with the people of Johnville for the Christmas celebration.

The mass was a time of reflection for Kate, looking back over the past seven years. It was strange to remember why she had left and how fate had led her on such a journey. She no longer felt any bitterness toward Simon, only sadness. Married life was apparently not for her, but, on the other hand, she had the advantage of a free spirit and freedom to travel where few women dared to go. She was independent, wealthy and confident, and she did not have to answer to the demands of another. She rationalized all these thoughts, yet deep inside she knew that, in spite of everything, she was still in love with Simon Gallagher.

During the winter months that followed, Kate was the centre of the social scene in Johnville and Bath. Friends vied for the privilege of holding teas and quilting parties in her honour, and she was urged to recite stories of her experiences. How much gold is there, really, in the Yukon? they asked. Did she own a mine of her own? Was it true that the snow was twenty feet deep? No one would believe her when she told them there was more snow outside in Johnville than she had ever seen in Whitehorse. In her good-humoured way, and always with a twinkle in her eye, she told of the trail to Teslin City, of the men and women she had met and of the experiences she had endured. The tale of the miner using a shovel for a collection plate in Reverend Pringle's tent church was a favourite, but there was never an end to the demands for her stories about the Yukon. Kate enthralled her audience with descriptions of the grandeur of the mountains, the rivers abounding in giant fish, the aurora borealis that sounded like a taffeta dress rustling in the northern sky. As she regaled her old friends and neighbours with stories about her new home, she realized how much she had become a part of the north and how strongly it was drawing her back.

For a few months, Kate felt obliged to help her brother John and his family. John's wife Nellie was expecting her second child, and John could barely make ends meet. In his attitude toward work, he resembled his father, never content with his job, always full of one grand scheme after another, but with little profit to show for his efforts. Nellie was a frail woman who said little, accepting her lot in life without complaint or comment. She recited the rosary daily, waited on her husband hand and foot and never questioned any of his efforts or lack thereof. John could help Pat and Anne Ryan very little, and Kate urged her parents to return with her to the Yukon. She now had the financial resources to make a comfortable home for them, but they refused her offer, feeling that at their ages they couldn't uproot their lives. John wanted to go north but kept putting it off. His second son, Leo, was born in April, barely ten months younger than his brother Bob. Kate took care of the frail infant and acted as his godmother. Holding the little boy in her arms as the priest put salt on his lips and water on his head, Kate felt a strong bond with the child. Little did she realize just how much a part of her life the delicate boy would become.

Spring came to Johnville with much the same fanfare as it did in the Yukon; the ice ran in the river and the streams flooded their banks. The warm sun drew Kate back to the hills behind the farm, and she explored the secret places of her childhood. But, as she looked out over the valley, she realized it was time for her to leave. This was no longer her home; her home was far away in the Yukon, and she made herself ready to return. John told his sister he would join her there, but he would wait until Nellie was stronger. In the meantime, they agreed that Kate would take the oldest baby, Bob, home with her, and Nellie would recuperate before the rest of the family made the long trip to Whitehorse. As for Bob, he was too young to have any say in the matter, but the decision proved so traumatic for him that he never forgave nor forgot it.

On March 25, 1902, a few weeks before Kate's return home, Major Snyder locked up a small woman in the Whitehorse jail. As part of the police attempt to crack down on the soubrettes, gamblers and known criminals entering the Yukon, the detachment received advance reports on all aliens known to be in the area, just in case. The dossier on Kitty Henry detailed her life and accomplishments thus far. She had earned a colourful reputation with the law on both sides of the border, and was now attempting to enter the Yukon illegally. The report read: “Eluded sentry at Whitehorse Rapids, illegal alien. Personal details, next of kin; Mother Kate Henry. Height 5’1/2“, weight 120 pounds. Residence, Minneapolis, Minnesota. Marital Status, widow. Age, 26 years, 3 months. Hair, tar brown. Personal features, small, quiet, nose top tilted. Followed mining camps, Stevens, Cripple Creek. Soubrette and prostitute. Crime, solicitation and solicitation. Sentence, one month hard labour.”

Thirty days was an unusually harsh sentence compared to the regular fines and overnight stays in jail meted out to most of the clients of the Whitehorse jail. Perhaps violence was involved, but, in any case, this lady must have “scalped” her customers in good fashion to earn such a sojourn in the Whitehorse lock-up. No one bailed her out, and she made no noteworthy attempt to escape. Instead, she bided her time, no doubt counting the days before she would be able to head to Dawson. But on the final day of her incarceration, the police ultimatum spoiled her scheme; she received a “blue slip.” She would be deported and put on the train the next morning for the outside. Kate may have been home in time to make an impression upon the woman in the cell, and perhaps she helped the North West Mounted Police constable escort Kitty Henry to the station and onto the train.

Little Bob added to Kate’s pleasure in the warm days of summer, but he also added to her work and worry. She had not been home very long when she was stricken with a severe case of shingles. The new doctor, Dr. Sugden, tried to talk her into letting him admit her to the rather rudimentary hospital, where she could be looked after properly, but she refused because she felt she could not leave the baby. With the help of friends and neighbours, she slowly recovered, but it was September before she was well enough to resume her job at the Whitehorse Hotel.

Although the mad rush of the golden days subsided in Whitehorse and the settlement began to take on the existence of a pioneer town, there was always that lingering spark that only needed to be fanned by the word “gold” to burst into flames. The cost of extracting gold caused an economic shift in the Yukon as large corporations took over most of the mining operations. Small investors sold their shares, and the new owners were absentee landlords who sent crew bosses and modern machinery to operate the mines. If life in the north did not produce material wealth for the pioneers, the men and women who shared in the experience of opening the Yukon seemed destined to be wiser because of the harsh realities of life and nature that they endured. In the outside world, they remained a tangible representation of the glorious times of "the '98."

With the scare of the rebellion a long way behind them, the government officials in Ottawa felt it was no longer necessary to maintain such a large and costly police force in Dawson and Whitehorse. But Zachary T. Wood, the Assistant Commissioner of the North West Mounted Police in the Yukon, disagreed and asked for more recruits. Government demands had increased their work. The police were responsible not only for enforcing the law and maintaining order; they also had to guard thousands of dollars in gold and monitor the constantly changing transient population. The new government laws prohibited faro, roulette and craps but permitted blackjack and poker. The prostitutes ordered out of Dawson just moved to Klondike City. For awhile the music halls remained open, but the Dawson town council passed an ordinance prohibiting dancing in licensed premises and preventing women from selling drinks on commission. The conflicting laws intended to control the vices of the times added to the work imposed on Wood and his shrinking contingent. Wood wrote to Ottawa to explain that his men, already facing these problems, could not also do a satisfactory job of collecting royalties on the gold leaving the territory.

Anyone taking gold out of the Yukon was supposed to pay a royalty tax on it. Then the owner would receive a certificate from the comptroller's office as proof that the tax was paid. Anyone carrying gold who was unable to show this certificate to the Canadian customs inspector at the Canada-U.S. boundary had to pay up or forfeit the gold. In the first years of the gold rush, the tax rate was set at 10%, but, thanks to the rebellion, the rate was lowered to 2.5%. Ironically, gold in the form of jewellery was not subject to the tax. Jewellers in Whitehorse and Dawson enjoyed a booming business creating fashionable medallions and ornaments in all shapes and sizes.

In his sessional reports to Ottawa, Wood continued to complain that his small force could not possibly collect this royalty tax efficiently, and he argued that the extra revenue that could be collected on the gold now being smuggled out of the country would more than compensate for the slight expense incurred by hiring extra custom officials. In a letter dated July 11, 1903, he wrote, "People . . . may carry out dust in their pockets or concealed on their persons. . . . To prevent this it would be necessary to have male and female examiners and rooms where they could search all passengers." But, he went on, "as we are already fifty short of our authorized strength and men are leaving every day, I am obliged to reduce the number of detachments instead of increasing them. The men we want to keep will not remain at the present rate of pay."

Finally, after countless letters and requests, the thought of the loss of tax revenue inspired the officials in Ottawa to take some action. They issued an order creating a post for a female gold inspector. On the recommendation of Fitz Horrigan and Phillip Primrose, Kate was given the position, and two weeks before her thirty-fourth birthday, the Commissioner of the Yukon officially appointed her Constable Special attached to "H" Division of the North West Mounted Police, Whitehorse.

In his next sessional report, Superintendent Snyder described how Kate and the constables assigned to work with her searched for gold dust. "Two constables and a woman special are detailed at Whitehorse for duty to search baggage and passengers for gold dust being smuggled out of the country. This duty is both arduous and unpleasant and a great deal of credit is due to constables detailed for this duty, for the tact and judgement used in carrying it out." Kate was described as "warmhearted, affable and efficient, the very woman for the job. She rarely has trouble with travellers, but is always supported by at least one constable who remains in the background unless required." Kate's companion and assistant during her first months of duty was Constable Michael Dooley. For the convenience of train travellers, they would ride the morning train out of Whitehorse "searching passengers, their baggage, etc.," with Miss Ryan in charge of "the persons and baggage of all women passengers." Before they reached the Alaska border, Kate, Constable Dooley and their helper would get off the Skagway-bound train and return home on the evening train to Whitehorse.

Late in August, an American steamer tied up at the Whitehorse wharf, and Kate boarded it to carry out her customs inspection. The steamer carried a group of American military personnel and their wives heading outside after a tour of duty in Alaska. Kate had fashioned herself a uniform that gave her a professional appearance, and her presence intrigued the America service wives. She moved among the group with authority, yet maintained her pleasing manner. She asked the women individually whether they carried any gold dust or nuggets that they wished to declare. Off to the side, one woman remained aloof and haughty, trying to avoid Kate and her questions. The lady's dress and manner identified her as a person of position and one used to asserting herself. Kate continued to do her job among the women and answer their questions about her unique position. After everyone else had been inspected, Kate approached the reluctant woman.

"Do you have any gold you wish to declare?" Kate asked.

The lady feigned contempt, and Kate repeated the request for information. "I'm sorry, Madam, but if you do not answer the questions, you will have to be searched."

"Oh, scarcely," replied the indignant woman. "Do you know to whom you are speaking? I am the wife of Major General Gerald Brompton, of the United States Army."

"And I, Madam," Kate answered firmly, "am myself an officer of the British Crown. Would you kindly step into the cabin."

Mrs. Brompton was about to refuse when Dooley stepped to her side and without a word directed her toward the cabin door. Left alone with Kate, she reluctantly uncoiled her chignon and released several large gold nuggets, which Kate promptly confiscated. The story spread around Whitehorse before Kate and Dooley got off the steamer. As Kate made her way home, Don Muirhead, the new station agent, greeted her. "A good evening to you, Miss Sergeant Kate," Don said, chuckling as he ducked out of the way before she could give him a good-natured swat on the back. Once again she was saddled with a second nickname, "Sergeant Kate."

Her new job, her other part-time work and the child filled her days to capacity. John and Nellie did not come to the Yukon as planned because Nellie was expecting another baby. John came alone the next spring, but he stayed only through the short summer and then returned to Johnville. Bob was growing and healthy, but for one reason or another they decided to leave him with his aunt.

On March 23, 1903, the citizens of Whitehorse once more encountered Kitty Rockwell, by now a dance-hall queen. The alert station agent noticed her arrival and scribbled a note to Fitz Horrigan at the police barracks warning him that Kitty Rockwell was back in town. It had been a few years since any girls of Kitty's sort had headed into Dawson; most were going the other way. Although she arrived this time with a bit more caution and propriety than on her first visit to Whitehorse, her appearance created a stir. She walked from the station over to the Whitehorse Hotel, where she booked a night's lodging and passage on the morning stage to Dawson. When Fitz visited the lady and questioned her travel plans, she curtly told him she was going to Dawson to visit a friend.

Since Whitehorse had seen her last, Kitty Rockwell had prospered. In Victoria, she had joined the 173-member Savoy Theatrical Company, a burlesque and musical troupe, and with them she had arrived in Dawson in the fall of 1900. Her star rose so fast that, by Christmas Eve, she was dancing among the miners in a $1,500 Paris dress, wearing a tin crown illuminated with fifty lighted candles. While building her career as a dancer and soubrette, Kitty fell in love with Alexander Pantages, then a saloon waiter cheating his fortune out of the miners, and the two became lovers. Pantages soon resumed the theatrical trade he had left in San Francisco. Starting with the Orpheum Theatre in Dawson, he was to become one of the greatest theatre magnates of the times, but in 1902 he and Kitty left the Yukon to operate nickelodeons and similar entreprises in Seattle and Victoria. Early in 1903, Kitty confirmed in a diary entry revealed some time later that Pantages had urged her to go to Texas to make some money for their business ventures. Her search for investment money had brought her to seek a miner whom she had met during her Dawson days. She may or may not have actually gone to Texas, but she did get money in Dawson. She later testified that Pantages used the money she sent him from Dawson to purchase a theatre in Seattle. Kitty stayed in Dawson for only a few weeks before she left again for the outside.

In 1905, the Yukon heard the rest of Kitty Rockwell's story. After she returned to Seattle, Kitty discovered that Pantages had married Lois Mendenhall, an eighteen-year-old violinist who had actually appeared on vaudeville bills with Kitty, and whose well-established Oakland, California family considered Pantages a secure if somewhat tarnished businessman. Kitty was enraged. On May 26, 1905, she filed a $25,000 breach-of-promise suit in the superior court of Kings County, Seattle, against Alexander Pantages.

The slightest hint of connection to anyone of gold rush fame attracted droves of newspaper reporters. A stage professional, Kitty made a grand appearance in the court room. Her case made headlines around the globe with her tales of her love affair with Alexander Pantages during their glory days in the Klondike. The newspapers revelled in every scrap of Kitty's sordid tale of her affair with Pantages and her descriptions of how they had worked the Dawson saloons and gambling establishments together. Kitty seemed to hold the strong hand. She had a number of love letters, and also Pantages had made a lot of enemies while making his fortune; many of these would be glad to testify against him. Her lawyers presented Pantages with a list of questions that clearly implicated him with the soubrette and documented their cohabitation in Dawson and the liaison that continued in San Francisco, Seattle and several small towns in the American mid-west. The hearings dragged on until fall, titillating the world with allegations and countercharges. Kitty was suing for financial compensation, Pantages was rich and the lawyers on both sides, who had taken the case on a contingency basis, were confident of a sizeable settlement. But just as it became evident that Kitty would win her suit, she signed a dismissal and left the state. Furious lawyers on both sides cried foul and took legal action of their own. By signing the dismissal, the notorious Kitty Rockwell had deprived them of the killing they had planned to make in legal fees. Once again, Kitty and her erstwhile lover were hauled back into court to make still more sensational revelations. Finally, the following spring, the

Kate Rockwell (Canapress Photo Service)

court cleared Pantages of the breach-of-promise charge in return for a property settlement. The amount was never made public, but rumours suggested that it ranged from $5,000 to $60,000. The lawyers never did find out just how much Kitty had been given to skip town.

At first, Kate Ryan was oblivious to the lawsuit and the stories being printed in American papers. Then she received an urgent telegram from Frank Burd, now a reporter on a Vancouver paper. "What is the law suit all about?" Others inquired if Kate was in some kind of trouble and needed help. Kate could not discover the source of the stories until finally Frank sent her clippings from the Seattle and San Francisco papers. "Klondike Kate Sues Pantages; Dance Hall Queen of the Yukon Sues Her Lover." Kate Ryan had little defense against something of which she had no knowledge and over which she had no control. All she could do was to write to her family and reassure them that the "Klondike Kate" referred to in the newspaper accounts was a one-time Dawson dance-hall girl who had no connection with her or with the name "Klondike Kate." This did not stop the confusion between Kate Ryan and this other "Klondike Kate." As the lawsuit dragged on and the story became more and more sensational, Kate tried to dissociate herself from the title altogether. But the confusion between herself and Kitty Rockwell caused by their common nickname continued to plague her. Those who knew her pioneering and her good works defended her, while the chroniclers of the saga of the Yukon gold rush often conflated the stories of these two very dissimilar personalities. Kate's family asked, "How did that 'other woman' take Kate's name?" They and Kate had to bear the burden of the headlines and sensational stories, and the "other woman" became a skeleton in the family closet.

Robert Service's Whitehorse Nights

In *1904, spring and summer* blended into one. The snow vanished and green hills appeared overnight. The mountains and river banks blossomed with tall sweet grass and fireweed, and the distant hills were spotted with flowers of the most delicate shades of yellow and fuchsia. The river released the great slabs of ice and as they fled the country they were replaced by steamers loaded with supplies and an incoming tide of workers and absentee landlords. Tourists, salesmen and miners flooded into the north to resume their business for the brief respite before the unrelenting ice returned, cramming a normal year's production into five months. The mines operated at full capacity day and night. Machinery worked constantly to dredge wealth from the earth. 1904 brought the opening of the Kluane district, an area rich in placer gold, and new mines started operations all around the area. Strikes were made at Bullion, Ruby, Sheep Camp, Kimberly and Fourth of July. Businessmen were elated that the mines showed such potential, and the discovery of a copper belt within ten miles of Whitehorse confirmed everyone's belief that the north had just begun to discover its natural wealth. Stroller White, the new editor of the Whitehorse *Star*, wrote, "No town in the far north could see a brighter star of hope and progress than their town and the economic future of Whitehorse would be greater than all the years of the past."

The first official day of spring was May 24, Queen Victoria's Birthday. Just in case any adult should forget, the school children chanted their favourite verse,

> The twenty-fourth of May is the Queen's Birthday!
> If we don't get a holiday we will all run away!

In response to the children's song, the North Star Athletic Club planned a day of celebration. With the first morning light

Kate (far left) and friends celebrating Victoria Day in Whitehorse, 1906. (KMK)

the citizens of Whitehorse opened their doors to welcome the midnight sun back into the north. They invited their American neighbours at Skagway to share in the day's festivities, with the understanding the Skagway group would reciprocate on Independence Day, July 4. The train arrived filled to capacity with friends and neighbours from Skagway and along the rail line, accompanied by musicians and the ball team, which had been challenged to a match by the Athletic Raiders.

The parade began at the railway station, led by the North West Mounted Police dressed in their brilliant uniforms and mounted on their splendid horses. The Whitehorse band followed the prancing horses, and the music echoed throughout the town. The Order of Yukon Pioneers, with their bright sashes and brilliant medallions gleaming in the sun, followed the band in close step. Next came the Athletic Club members, waving their banners high overhead to the delight of the cheering onlookers. Behind the Athletic Club marched the town's pride and joy, the Athletic Raiders, all decked out in the uniforms purchased especially for this new season. The parade was fortified by the members of the IODE, followed by the school children proudly waving their Union Jacks in time to the music. The group wound its way down Main Street and over to the ball field for the highlight of the afternoon, the ball game between the Athletic Raiders and the Skagway Marauders.

The spirited game led to side bets and wagers. Those in the bleachers cheered their support for the team of their choice, until finally a tie game was called by the umpire. The hungry townspeople and their guests hurried over to the club rooms for a picnic supper laid on by the IODE and the Athletic Club women. Most of the women belonged to both associations, so each cooked double and the tables groaned with food. Festooned with spring bouquets and bunting, Her Royal Highness Queen Victoria smiled down from her oval frame, no doubt basking even in heaven in the joy of her people in the Yukon.

There was little time for anything but work during the summer months. The town kept up a frantic pace. Everyone planted gardens, which grew at a phenomenal rate under the long hours of daylight. They constructed new homes and businesses, fished in the streams and rivers filled with an abundance of trout and Arctic char, and enjoyed the fruits of nature. In late September the human tide began to ebb again, and the same group that had come on the spring boats now hurried toward the steamers for their fall voyage to the outside. After the last run of the season, the steamers docked, the river iced over and the season came to an abrupt close. With the "cheechakos" gone, the true sourdoughs took over and the real life of the Yukon began.

Whitehorse settled down for the winter, and in late November a rather insignificant-looking young man arrived on the White Pass and Yukon train. As he stepped down from the coach, the thought struck him that he had come to a "racoon convention" — everyone on the platform wore a long racoon coat, the most elegant fashion of the day. He was greeted by Harold Taylor, the teller at the Bank of Commerce, whom the manager had dispatched to greet the new clerk, Robert Service. From the day he arrived in Whitehorse, Service found himself drawn into the social life of the town. He described the time as one of the happiest of his life. He was a shy young man, reluctant to get involved, but, urged by Taylor and his fellow workers, he found himself at the skating rink and the dances with Whitehorse society. He soon learned about the two social classes, the respectable establishment and the denizens of Lousetown. Of the people who were to become his friends, he wrote, "The wild brings out virtues we do not find easily in cities — brotherhood, sympathy, high honesty. As if to combat the harshness of nature, human nature makes an effort to be at its best." He found these virtues among the northern pioneers. Secluded from the outside world, they settled down to share with each other the best possible life they could make.

Whitehorse people spent every effort to make each undertaking, whether social or business, a success. No one ever needed to feel left out or lonely; everyone was made welcome. Even a shy bank clerk was expected to participate and was gently forced to join the life that surrounded him. All of the important functions took place at the North Star Athletic Club, which boasted a handball court and a meeting hall large enough to play baseball in. At least one night a week that hall was used for community whist games. When visitors entered the Club, they were met at the door by one of the patronesses, Mrs. G.A. Pringle, Mrs. M.J. Taylor or Miss Kate Ryan, who made everyone feel perfectly at home. Apart from the Club, there were hospital meetings and council meetings to attend, the fire brigade held regular get-togethers and of course the churches sponsored many events. The skating rink was always a scene of gaiety and glamour, where young men met their girls and waltzed on the crisp ice under the grandeur of the Northern Lights. If all this was not enough, the town sports could enjoy the thrills of the toboggan slide or the excitement of the curling matches.

The most popular events of all were the weekly dances. Each dance had a different theme — the Valentine Ball, a Costume Ball, a Sourdoughs' Dance or a Calico Ball — and each was a "proper time" where no one carried liquor. Stroller White wrote up the dances with great delight in the Whitehorse *Star*. "Excellent music, a good floor and congenial associates," he would say. "What more could one desire to pass a pleasant and enjoyable evening? . . . It was a matter of no surprise to everyone who attended the fancy dress ball given by the Athletic Club on the evening of the 18th to see so many beautiful costumes and well-sustained characters. It was the most largely attended evening in

Robert Service (back row, right) and friends after a dinner celebrating the publication of *Songs of a Sourdough*, Dawson, 1908. (NAC)

the social history of Whitehorse." Stroller genially recorded the winners of all the prizes for "the most comical," "the best waltzer," "the best sustained gentleman" or "the cake walk," and announced the prizes: a box of cigars, a large cake, a small cake, a stick pin, a ham sandwich or a piece of pie. At the Fancy Dress Ball, Kate won a prize as the best lady waltzer, and on another occasion she and Norman Macauley were awarded a consolation prize in the way of a ham sandwich. A great deal of thought and planning went into every event. The ladies met in committee to solicit the food while the men collected prizes from the local business establishments. Robert Service described the dances he attended. "There was enough inebriation in the air without the stimulus of alcohol. The girls danced divinely for all Yukoners excelled in the art. The men learned in the dance halls, while the women were just naturally light on their toes."

Kate was at the peak of her life. She continued her ceaseless work, but, even with her heavy schedule, she managed to belong to the Catholic Women's League, the Hospital Committee, the North Star Athletic Club, the IODE and the Liberal Association. A leader in her community, she was surrounded by friends, and among the closest were Norman Macauley, Bob Lowe, Pat Brennan and Minnie Lamereau. At 35 years of age, Kate remained among the most popular of the "young ladies" in town. Her little house behind the Bank of Commerce continued to be a gathering place for all to drop in for a chat or a cup of tea. Harold Taylor brought over the new bank clerk, and soon he too made a habit of stopping by. The trail of '98 was a long way behind for Kate and most of her friends, but, once story-telling began, everyone had something to offer about the trails they had shared. No one realized that Robert Service would one day etch their stories into history. He had not been in the Yukon himself during the gold rush, and newspapers later claimed that he got many of his stories from Kate herself. But Kate was more modest about her contribution. She admitted to one reporter that Service had retold some of her experiences, and she told another, "I suppose I did supply him some incidents which he subsequently wove into certain of his poems. But I was by no means the only one to do so." Service's ballads immortalize the tales he heard from the veterans of '98 in Kate's living room.

Service remained in Whitehorse for two years, and during that time few people realized that he wrote poetry. Stroller White encouraged the new writer and had even published his poem "The Little Old Log Cabin" in 1902, before Service came north. When the Athletic Club organized a talent show, Stroller encouraged Service to recite one of his own verses, but instead Service reluctantly read a verse from some other author and kept his own words to himself. He did, however, confide in Kate, because she had one asset that was of great help to him: she could type. From time to time, she would rent a typewriter from the Mounted Police detachment and type out fair copies for him. Years later, Kate admitted that she still had some of Service's manuscripts, as well as a copy of the first edition of Robert Service's first book of poetry.

When Service sent his work to a publishing company, he never imagined that anyone would want to buy his poems. He thought he would get only the 100 copies that he ordered and expected to pay for himself. These 100 books arrived in Whitehorse on the first supply steamer in the spring, along with a request for permission to print his poetry for sale and an advance royalty payment. Beaming with pride, Service gave copies to his closest friends, those who had encouraged his writing. With the publication of the second edition of *The Spell of the Yukon*, the world outside revelled in the ballads of Robert Service, while in Whitehorse the actual Sam McGee would not speak to "that damned whipper-snapper" and crossed the street when he saw Service coming. Sam swore that Service did not tell the story the way the "cremation" really happened, but the world didn't care. Readers loved Service's rendition, and as with many stories of the north, truth gathered dust as the world begged to hear the ballad of "The Cremation of Sam McGee" again and again.

The greatest fear of any town in the early 1900's was not of natural disaster but of a man-made disaster, fire. The main business section of Whitehorse consisted of wooden frame buildings, and the catastrophe in Dawson in 1899 taught everyone a grim lesson. The Whitehorse Citizens' Council tried to protect their thriving community from fire. In 1901 they built a fire hall, and in 1904 they added water tanks and hired an engineer to maintain the tanks and the town's fire equipment. During the early hours of a spring morning in 1905, the dreaded clamour of the fire bell jerked the townspeople from their beds — the White Pass Hotel was on fire. In his autobiography, *Ploughman of the Moon*, Robert Service gives a vivid account of the conflagration started by this small fire. The hotel guests fled into the street in their night clothes, and the volunteer firemen ran to the pumphouse just a few hundred yards from the hotel. The men shouted in panic as they searched for the engineer, but his cabin was empty and the keys to the pumphouse couldn't be found. Just as the men began to ram the door, the dishevelled engineer came running from the direction of Lousetown. Finally, the men attacked the fire with pumps and hoses. The frightened engineer hid out of sight lest the angry crowd turn their fury on him. Breathlessly, the crowd waited for the stream of water to quell the flames shooting out of the roof of the hotel. At last, the hoses filled and water streamed into the air. After an eternity, the fire appeared to

The fire at Whitehorse, May 23, 1904, as it raged through the main section of town. (KMK)

be under control. Suddenly, flames appeared in the back of the hotel, shooting up like fireworks into the night sky. The men hurried around the hotel, dragging their hoses behind them. To their horror, just as they began to attack the second burst of flames, the water stopped — they had pumped the tanks dry. The incompetent engineer had allowed the water to get low, and there was no water left to fight the raging fire. With their only resort being rain barrels and brave bucket brigades, the people of Whitehorse fought the fire. Frail women became amazons, and strong men panicked, saving worthless produce and leaving valuable records behind. Young and old alike took their place in the bucket lines, as men led horses from stables while mothers searched frantically for lost children. The fire continued to devastate the town into the predawn hours, and it was early morning before the fire burned itself out. Surveying the wreckage of their town, the inhabitants realized that the business section had been virtually wiped out. The only buildings spared were the government buildings and the ones owned by outside companies. The community that the day before had been happy and secure was now a pile of charred rubble.

Northerners were used to hardships, and almost immediately they began setting up tents and operating their businesses the way they had when they first came to the Yukon. Kate lost her little cabin, but, like her neighbors, she made plans to build again. An army of carpenters came in on the spring steamers. Kate's new home was a two story building with a "store front" on the first floor and an upstairs apartment. She rented the front, and she and her nephew moved into the apartment, making plans for the arrival of her brother John and his family. John Ryan arrived in Whitehorse after the fire and left at freeze-up, promising to return the next year with the rest of his family. But tragedy struck the Ryan family again with the death of John's wife Nellie. Not only was Bob without a mother, but the younger boys at home in Johnville had no one to take care of them. John returned the following spring, and this time he brought John, Jr. and Leo, Kate's godchild. In July, 1909, the fourth brother, Charlie, joined the family in Whitehorse. Jerry Quinlan, the conductor on the White Pass and Yukon train, had married a Miss McCormick from Woodstock, New Brunswick. Mrs. Quinlan's sister, Elizabeth McCormick, travelled all the way from Woodstock to visit her sister in Whitehorse, and she brought Charlie with her to join Kate's household.

Kate's new home overflowed with the addition of her brother and the boys. The baby of the family, Walter, remained in Johnville with the McAdam family and never made the trip to the Yukon; consequently, he knew very little about the life of his brothers. Always restless, John Ryan made several trips back and forth across the country. He started horse trading, which suited his fancy, succeeded in this work for a time, and seemed to produce a fair bit of wealth. He dabbled a bit in the mines, and after his last trip north, he seemed to be "well off" by Johnville standards. By the time the younger boys came to Whitehorse, Bob was growing to be a good-sized lad and an able worker. He found the strain of being separated from his family hard to bear, and the sudden death of his mother, a woman he never knew, left a terrible burden on the child. Life seemed to him work and more work, even as a little boy. When he was old enough, he left the north to finish his schooling in Bath, New Brunswick, where he joined his father's horse-trading business, which finally

The Ryan boys (from left to right): Bob, Leo, John Jr., Charlie

(Annie Brennan Guest)

led him to the United States. He never returned to the north; with a heavy heart, he always said it was a terrible life for a child. The three middle boys, Leo, John Jr. and Charlie, remained in the north with Kate. Their aunt was the only mother the children could ever remember.

Kate now had a full house and a family to support, and she still had the investments that took her away on short excursions to inspect the mines. The profits were a godsend now that she had all the extra mouths to feed. The boys began to attend school as they grew old enough, but they were not scholars. Kate had all she could do to keep them at their books long enough so they could at least read and write. They were far more interested in horses and in the outside world.

Kate continued her work at the customs, but she was rarely called upon to act as matron at the jail. In spite of their professional enmity, she remained on cordial terms with the Lousetown ladies. One of the most notable of these was a woman known as Roma Dean. Roma was among the first of the bar-room ladies to arrive in Whitehorse with her own entourage of female employees. She was not a common saloon girl; she was a shrewd business woman and a high-class prostitute. Roma and her girls had won notoriety on their journey upriver to Whitehorse. The steamer on which they were travelling ran aground on a sandbar on an inner channel along the coast. The frenzied crew shouted commands and curses, but the boat remained high and dry, stuck until the next tide. From the shore came whistles and catcalls from wood-cutters waiting to load the steamer with firewood. With the unexpected stop, Roma and her girls started a grand promenade on the deck, with all the dramatics and fanfare of their profession. Never one to miss a business opportunity, Roma shouted her orders for all to hear: "Scatter y're arse, and pay your way." The girls hiked up their dresses and waded ashore. From that day on, the sandbar was known as "Scatter Y're Arse Bar," until a high-minded government geographer in the 1940's changed its name. His intervention erased "Scatter Y're Arse" from the navigation charts and eliminated Roma Dean's claim to immortality.

Their reputation preceded Roma and her girls to Whitehorse. Never pretentious, they set up shop at first in a large tent, where they sold booze and other amenities at the inflated prices of the day. Roma soon acquired a lot of money and a silent partner, a man willing to invest in one of the most lucrative businesses in town. Like others, Roma moved her operation into a frame building in Lousetown as soon as she could. She saw to it that her girls had their fines paid promptly, and she seemed to treat them fairly. Her business sense kept them all living well, and her manner, if not socially acceptable, at least allowed her business to be tolerated within the limits of the law. But, in spite of her calculating manner and callous ways, she had two weaknesses, one that was public knowledge and a second that she confided to only one person and then only because she believed she was about to die.

Everyone in Whitehorse knew of Roma's fondness for liquor. When she went on a binge she was a holy terror. Her semi-annual spree always ended in some sort of brawl, she would land in jail and Fitz Horrigan would send for Kate, for as soon as the constable had locked her up, Roma would begin bawling and shouting for Kate. Between the medicine that Doc Sugden would give her and some soft consoling, Kate would finally quiet her down. After a few days of recuperation, the sober

Roma would vow to reform, with promises to Kate that she would return to church, and guarantees to Fitz Horrigan that she would never touch a drop of liquor again. Full of remorse and good intentions, Roma would leave jail and go back to her business until the next time.

Roma's second weakness surfaced during the Whitehorse measles epidemic. The *Star* reported that a number of persons were confined because of a serious outbreak of measles in the district, but the comment in the social news on the plight of Roma Dean didn't tell half the story. "Roma Dean, a member of the demimonde, had been ill with measles and pneumonia, and at one time chances for her recovery were slim, but she is now slowly improving." When Roma caught the infectious disease, Doc Sugden realized that she must be quarantined to protect the public, and he asked Kate if she would consider taking care of a rather questionable patient. Kate laughed at the thought of Roma as a house guest and asked Doc only one question, "Is she sober?" Roma's condition was very grave indeed when her girls brought her to Kate's home. Kate prepared a separate room for Roma to keep her away from the rest of the family. Two of the boys had already had the measles, and Kate sent the third one to stay with neighbors until the epidemic was over. Roma was too sick to protest her confinement at Kate's house, and wandered in and out of consciousness as the fever raged. Both Kate and Doc Sugden thought she was going to die, and so did Roma herself. During a conscious period, she begged Kate to send word to Big Alex the Swede that she wanted to see him before she died. The request surprised Kate, but she could not deny Roma her dying wish, so she sent one of the boys to hunt for the Big Swede.

Everyone in town knew Big Alex Gustavson. A tall, angular man with square shoulders, he had the strength of Atlas. He had a small mine a few miles out in the bush, but he came into town often for supplies. A popular man, he had a fetish about his personal appearance and was always carefully groomed. When he came to town, he headed first for the bath house and then to the barber shop. His pride and joy was his beautiful waxed handlebar moustache, which he twisted and turned as he spoke. Like many of the men of the bush, he had a weakness for the devil spirits, and when he was drunk a wise man kept out of his way.

It was common knowledge that Alex had a battle with Charlie Lund over ownership of some cattle. As the argument reached serious proportions, Big Alex was seen heading out towards his camp one day driving a herd of cattle. When the constable finally caught up to him and ordered him to take Charlie Lund's herd back, Alex presented the facts as he saw them. "Dat cow she saw me going an' by dang she just jumped the fence to follow." The judge heard so much conflicting evidence from both Charlie and Alex that, feeling some sympathy for Alex, he fined him $5 and let him go. Unhappy with this outcome, Charlie boasted around town that he would get even with Alex. A few people thought that Charlie was the money behind Roma's Palace, and many also speculated that Charlie had cheated the Swede out of a mining claim. With the court settlement against Charlie, the town waited for the two men to settle their own dispute.

Alex received Kate's message to stop by her house. When he arrived, Kate explained that Roma Dean lay in the next room, so ill with the measles that Doc Sugden thought she was near death. Kate had sent for Alex because Roma wanted to confide in him before she died. If Alex was shocked he did not show it, and he agreed to talk to the woman. Big Alex had been the only man that was ever able to soften Roma Dean's callous heart, and she wanted to tell him of her love before she departed into the hereafter. On the pretext of an errand, Kate left the house for a short time, and when she returned Alex was gone. Not long afterwards, Roma rallied, her fever broke and Doc Sugden allowed that she might survive after all. Within a few days, Roma got up from her deathbed and moved back to her Palace across the tracks, without speaking of her visitor. She never mentioned Alex's visit again and Kate never mentioned it either. The matter appeared to be closed.

One Saturday some months later, Alex returned to town. He made his usual rounds, cashing in his gold (which some said was a considerable amount), buying his supplies, and then, as was his habit, stopping at the hotel for a bath before his trip to the barber shop. By early evening, Alex was ready for Roma's Palace across the tracks. Roma's place of business now had an extension on the back and a second story. The two rooms at the back served as Roma's private quarters and office, while the upstairs was reserved for the girls and their guests. When Alex entered the saloon the room reeked of wood smoke, human bodies and stale beer. He made his way through the crowd and ordered a drink. After about half an hour, Alex was posed with his back to the curtained door that led to Roma's office. Without warning, Charlie Lund stepped from behind the curtain and struck Alex on the back of the head. In an instant, the whole place was in an uproar. Tables were overturned, glasses smashed on the floor and women screamed as the room filled with shouts and curses. For a moment Alex staggered forward, then regained his balance and turned to face his assailant. The two men struggled and groaned as they threw punch after punch at one another. Alex appeared to have the upper hand, but Charlie, who never stopped for an honourable fight, threw a kick to Alex's groin. As the huge Swede doubled over in pain, Charlie grabbed at his magnificent handlebar moustache. When the two men separated, blood spurted from Alex's face as a jagged lip dangled from the side of his mouth.

Suddenly, as if on a signal, the lanterns were snuffed out. Alex fumbled for his opponent in the dark, but instead he felt a hand in his leading him through the curtained door and out into the winter's night. The sharp cold air cleared his drunken senses. He reached into his pocket to retrieve a large cotton handkerchief which he pressed to his lip to staunch the gushing blood. Shaking his head, he reached into his pocket again and realized that what was left of his gold poke was gone. The lights were on again in the saloon, and the music and noise rose as he stood outside alone. The moon lifted itself carefully over the hills as he lurched across town and behind the fire hall and the post office, followed only by the sound of his feet crunching in the snow. He did not notice the crimson trail that followed him as he staggered past the bank and through the alley. He mounted the steps of the frame house and pounded on the door until his pounding brought a light from inside. Kate opened the door and stood in the shadow of her lamp. Without question, she drew him into the kitchen, and only there, in the brighter light, did she recognize her visitor. Johnny appeared from the bedroom, awakened by the commotion, and his aunt called for him to bring her medicine bag. Alex mumbled incoherently, but the few words she could understand told her that Charlie Lund had inflicted this terrible disfigurement on the Swede's handsome face.

"Dat Charlie, I'm going to kill him sure," Alex vowed, groaning with pain.

"Not tonight, Alex, not tonight", Kate cautioned. She assessed the wound and asked if he had any more of that hootch. From deep beneath the folds of his heavy mackinaw he produced a metal flask and placed it on the table.

"You had better take a good swig of that stuff, Alex," she ordered. "This is going to be quite a job."

She retrieved a rough grey blanket from the cot behind the stove and threw it over the kitchen table. By using a little gentle persuasion, she finally managed to get the drunken man down on the table. Her precious medical bag yielded catgut, scissors, alcohol, needles and bandages, and by this time the contents of his flask had put her patient in an amiable, talkative mood. With a few deft strokes, Kate removed the remainder of the glorious moustache and began to repair the jagged cut. While her patient stopped to finish the flask, Kate threaded the surgical needle with catgut. Once more she placed a firm hand on the big man and quickly attached the lip to its rightful position. The combination of the heat from the stove, the pain of the operation and the final drop of whiskey made Alex so docile that Kate could lead her towering patient like a child to the cot.

"You'll be fine in the morning, Alex," Kate soothed, "and don't worry, your moustache will grow back in no time."

Alex was more concerned that the loss of his poke meant he had no money with which to pay her, but Kate put him off with a scoff and covered him with a clean blanket. Before she had tidied up the kitchen and blown out the lantern, he was sound asleep. Kate awoke in the morning with a start as she remembered her patient. But she was surprised to find the kitchen empty. The only evidence of the night's encounter lay on the kitchen table. There, wrapped in a worn piece of blue velvet, lay an intricately-carved gold brooch.

Echoes of War

Like a spider, the war declared in Europe in August 1914 spread its web across the ocean, entangling even the inhabitants of the far northern territory. In Dawson, George Black recruited a volunteer band of men that became known as the Boyle and Black Contingent. The military force soon left the north, taking many of the able-bodied young men to the far shores of Europe. The train station at Whitehorse was a daily scene of separation, as mothers, wives and lovers saw their men board the train, knowing they might never see each other again. The glory of war was soon lost, as reports of death and injury began to filter back to the Yukon. In newspapers and letters, the men of the north wrote of the misery they suffered and of the wounding and death of comrades far away from the grandeur and peace of the Yukon.

In the second month of the war, Kate received word from Johnville that her cousin Joe Ryan was one of the first casualties. Another letter told that her dear friend John Pringle lost his own son in the trenches of France, and that he himself had gone to Europe. Pringle had accepted a call to Sydney, Nova Scotia, in 1909, but his crusading days had not ended. He did not surprise Kate by going into yet another battle for the Lord. The Whitehorse *Star* reported that George Pearkes, a Royal North West Mounted Police constable in Whitehorse in 1912 and 1913, had been severely wounded at Passchendaele. When Kate thought of George, she had to smile to herself, recalling her part in the brief love match between George and Irene Martin. The young policeman was moonstruck on Irene, but the rules of the force prevented any fraternizing between the men and the town girls. To add to George's dilemma, Irene's father, Ed Martin, was very strict with the bright-eyed young lady and watched over her like a hawk. George had coaxed Kate to let him use her parlour for a clandestine meeting, and she reluctantly consented. On the pretext of returning a borrowed pattern, Irene arrived at the appointed hour, and Kate escorted her into the parlour. A few minutes later George arrived, flustered and red-faced. Kate ushered him into the parlour, too, and busied herself in the kitchen, making a pot of tea and as much noise as possible. But, always one to be on the cautious side, and not one to leave much to chance, she placed a silver quarter in young Johnny's hand and winked.

"You keep an eye on the parlour, Johnny. We can never really be too careful with these young constables, can we?"

The young man never knew that his actions were monitored, but Kate gave him full marks for his gentlemanly conduct. Then, like thousands of other young men in love, he gave himself over to the war, and the romance ended. George left Canada for Europe and was soon commissioned as an officer. In October 1917 he led his men to the top of Passchendaele ridge. History records the events of that battle, and that George Pearkes survived his wounds and became a Canadian hero, decorated with the Victoria Cross for his bravery. After the war, he returned to Canada to become the federal Minister of Defense. He won decorations again in the Second World War, and following that he became Lieutenant-Governor of British Columbia.

While the war raged in Europe Kate continued her community work, feeling a tremendous burden to contribute all she could possibly manage to the war effort. She solicited funds, gathered knitted goods from the women of the IODE and sold Canadian Bonds with fervour. She maintained a perpetual rummage sale in her home, the proceeds of which she donated to the Canadian Red Cross Disablement Fund. The rummage sale almost ran itself. Kate was at work most of the time, but she never locked her door. She left the articles for sale in her living room, and buyers and contributors entered her home at will, dropped off goods for sale or purchased the goods they needed, and deposited payment in a can on the kitchen table. This sale continued for several years, and the Red Cross awarded Kate an honourary life membership for her efforts.

The North Star Athletic Club planned a wonderful celebration for New Year's, 1916. They wanted to bring some hope to their community, for the town seemed to receive harsh news from Europe every day. The new hospital, one of the Club's pet projects, had just been finished, and so they decided to hold the

New Year's Dance there before it opened. They had watched the idea grow from a drawing on a piece of paper to the fulfilment of their dreams, complete with the most modern hospital equipment. It was a tangible sign of their faith in their community, and they had every reason to be proud and optimistic about the future of their town.

Early on New Year's Eve, lights shone out of the hospital windows. Kate, Annie Taylor and Kluane Miller, along with the other members of the Hospital Auxiliary, bustled about making up sweet trays, arranging the winter greens and bells around the rooms. Oil lamps and paper streamers added to the gaiety, and the warmth from the new furnace filled the rooms. Kluane and Annie, the hostesses, met the guests at the door and escorted them to the dressing rooms, where they left their heavy outdoor clothes to display their New Year's finery. Excitement filled the air as the rooms filled with revellers inspecting every nook and cranny of the building. Room by room, they praised the fixtures and commended the workmanship. No one had ever seen such modern steel surgical tables and instruments, and they asked the doctors and nurses how such complicated equipment would be used.

The sound of the orchestra tuning up in the main room gathered the crowd together for the first waltz. First a Scottish reel, next a Virginia reel — the merry crowd whirled around the dance floor. Everyone joined in the cake walk, and no one sat out the grand march and circle. At midnight, the bells rang and the dancers held hands around the hall, bidding farewell to 1915 and welcoming 1916 with joyful exuberance. Each greeted his neighbour as the musicians played "Auld Lang Syne," and many offered a silent prayer that this year the war would end and all their loved ones would come home safely.

To dispel the momentary solemnity, the musicians picked up the pace of the music and led the crowd to the second floor, where the women had converted a hospital room into a banquet hall. There they found elegant tables laden with plates of cold chicken, rolls and sweets. Vases of artificial flowers and greens adorned the lace tablecloths, and candles flickered and danced. After supper, the guests proclaimed themselves unsatisfied and returned to the dance floor. The gentlemen of Whitehorse waltzed their ladies round and round until 1916 was three hours old. Then Bob Lowe escorted Kate to the cloak room to get their wraps, and with the rest of the merry-makers, they reluctantly wended their way homeward. Overhead the north star acted as a friendly beacon and the big dipper reached down close enough to touch.

The "cheechakos" who came to the north all had a vague sense of winter days that were all darkness. The hours of rich sunshine and absence of deep snow and wind always surprised them. And the darkness had a beauty of its own. The stars, near and vibrant, flashed colours of red, blue and green, and the lawless moon seemingly refused to take any regular path over the northern sky, rambling at will about the hills and trees. But the sight that converted all to the north was the orchestra of light that poured from the sky and echoed back from the snow-covered mountains, the Northern Lights. The colours of the hypnotic lights changed delicately, the fantastic roping movements dancing the perfect harmony of sky and earth. Legend had it that once a "cheechako" learned to turn to face the lights he would become a true Northerner.

Kate, Bob and the other dancers continued their waltz under the orchestra of light and sound of the Northern Lights, circling home in the happy certainty that 1916 would be a year they would all remember. It began as it should, with curling bonspiels, a Valentine dance, the Disablement Fund Dances, the IODE and Red Cross benefits. Kate was involved with all of the events and rarely missed organizing or at least participating. She collected more money for the War Effort than any other individual in the Yukon, and she received a special letter from the Prime Minister commending her for her hard work. When Kate's friends Rod Thomas and Jennie Shallow were married in Rod's new little house, Kate and Charlie Rowalinson acted as their witnesses. About her own single life, Kate would wisecrack, "always a bridesmaid and never a bride," but her ready-made family of three growing boys seemed to make marriage out of the question for her. Still, she often wondered if she ever would find someone to share her life.

Spring came, bringing the steamers back on their regular schedule and ushering in the hectic pace of summer. The

Princess Sophia brought some beef cattle to Skagway, and Ed Martin, the butcher, promised to have some good steak on the first train. School closed in June, freeing the Ryan boys of their books for the summer. They barely passed, but Kate was grateful for that small mercy. They were growing up and able to do a man's work, so they had little use for schooling.

The brief summer months flew by, the long daylight hours filled with jobs of every kind. September came and the steamers began to make their last runs of the year. The women returned to their social functions and formed a new association, the Yukon Women's Protective League, advocating the right to vote for the women of the north. Three looming problems goaded them into battle. First, the results of the previous election infuriated them. Over 1,700 votes had been cast despite the fact that, without the 400 men who had gone to war, there were only 1,300 eligible voters in the territory. The voters' lists were padded with foreigners who worked in the Yukon but who were not Canadian citizens, while they, the very founders and builders of the region, were denied the right to vote. The women decided they would not stand for this injustice; if necessary, they would fight for their democratic rights. The second bone of contention was "devil drink." Liquor ruled the chicanery of election day, since buying votes with a bottle of whiskey was not only acceptable but expected. The well-lubricated election celebrations poured salt in the wounds. On a wider front, the women saw the destruction wrought on their families and their communities by the evil powers of liquor. They shared in the surge of rebellion against alcohol by Canadian women everywhere, who suffered because of widespread drunkenness. The Yukon Women's Protective League demanded not only the vote but also harsh penalties for the sale of alcohol. And the War itself affected Canadian women. For the first time, women took part in business and industry, and the men in power could not deny the enormous contributions women at home made to support the troops. Clearly, the reconstruction of the country after the war would require help from all members of society, and the Yukon women wanted equal partnership in this rebuilding.

In outlying districts, small groups and individuals worked as hard as they could to bring about reform, and well-organized

Yukon Women's Protective League committees met in homes and church rooms in Dawson and Whitehorse. Because Kate's home was neutral territory for all social classes, the women of Whitehorse used it as a central office and meeting place. The women were adamant in their demands from the government in Ottawa. They wanted amendments that would eliminate the word "male" and "woman" from the Dominion Election Act, so that qualifications to vote would be the same for women as for men. Such an amendment would lift the mothers, wives and daughters of Canada from the degradation of being classed with idiots and criminals. This fight went on in all communities across the Dominion, but, unlike many men elsewhere, Yukon men generally supported the women's demands. The pioneer efforts to build the north left little room for prejudices. The Yukon women had long since proven their ability and strength in the face of adversity; these were not ladies of the drawing rooms, these were women who had climbed mountains.

The Whitehorse *Star* reported the meetings of the Yukon Women's Protective League in the light of the other dramatic events of the day. As women struggled for the right to vote, young men died in Europe to protect that right. Letters came from boys in boot camp longing for news of any kind from home. They were lonesome, homesick, hungry and afraid, and Robert Service expressed their feelings in "Tri-colour," a poem he wrote from a field in France:

> *Poppies*, you try to tell me, glowing there in the wheat;
> *Poppies*! Ah, no! You mock me: it's blood, I tell you, it's blood.
> It's gleaming wet in the grasses, it's glistening warm in the wheat;
> It dabbles the ferns and the clover, it brims like an angry flood;
> It leaps to the startled heavens, it smothers the sun, it cries
> With scarlet voices of triumph from blossom and bough and blade.
> See the bright horror of it! It's roaring out of the skies,
> And the whole red world is a-welter . . . Oh God! I'm afraid, I'm afraid.

The Sinking of the Princess Sophia

In *October, 1918,* newspapers across Canada spread hope that the war in Europe would soon be over. In the predawn light of October 23, they stamped out their headlines: "British Troops in Two Days Take 9,000 Prisoners, 150 Guns; French Advance — Capture 2,000." While history was being made in Europe, the people of Whitehorse were just waking up to a crisp fall morning. The shriek of the train whistle suddenly pierced the silence of the grey dawn, jarring Kate from a night of restless sleep. She arose reluctantly to face the day and what was before her. After weeks of discussion, she had finally consented to let Leo go home to New Brunswick with a shipment of horses. He was still a boy in her mind, barely sixteen, and she wanted him to stay, but he was determined to do a man's work and wanted to be treated like a man. Finally she had given in to his pleas.

She was grateful that Leo was not old enough to join the army; at least he would go to New Brunswick just for the winter, and he would be safe there. The boys were her life, and she could not imagine what she would do without them. She tried not to admit it, even to herself, but Leo remained her favourite. He was her godchild, and also he seemed to need protection more than the other two boys. He was tall, thin and handsome, physically a reflection of his father, but in many ways he had his mother's sensitivity. Kate worried about how he would manage in the harsh world. Going about her morning rituals, Kate could not shake her sense of foreboding. Her godson, on the other hand, could hardly contain his excitement — he was going outside. The second blast of the train whistle sounded her signal to leave for work. Putting on her uniform jacket, she closed the damper in the stove and shouted for the two younger boys to hurry. When the train pulled away from the station, many Yukoners would be on it, rushing to flee the north before freeze-up. Kate stepped out into the early morning, as she had for the past fifteen years. Her tall figure dressed in uniform gave her such an air of authority that men touched their caps as they hurried past. The town was on the move, their lives controlled by the train whistle.

People streamed towards the station, knowing that they must leave before it was too late. Otherwise, they would have to make themselves content with the solitary life of the long northern winter. Some, like Kate, had no desire to leave. They welcomed the isolation, they enjoyed the life of the small community and they revelled in the pleasures of the relaxed winter months. They went to the station to bid good-bye to friends, and then they looked forward to a quiet, sociable Whitehorse winter. Mothers hurried along pulling their sleepy children, adjusting their bonnets and straightened their ties, as they bustled towards the station. Old prospectors, drummers and smooth-shaven soldiers were all caught up in the pull towards the train. Kate stood at her customs inspection post when the hour whistle blew and her assistant, Corporal John Clifford, hurried down the platform to join her. In the distance, at the far end of the train, Kate could see Leo and his two brothers struggling with the horses as they tried to get them loaded into the livestock car.

Customs inspection had become a matter of routine after fifteen years, and the amount of gold being smuggled out had become very small, but the government still felt it necessary to continue presenting their authority in the north. During the early years, the imagination of the would-be smugglers had constantly amazed Kate. She found gold in hollowed-out bars of soap, nuggets in Bibles, nuggets stashed in hat bands and even gold sewed into corsets. Kate liked to tell about a young married couple who had come out of the Pelly district with a new baby. They had cleverly concealed a small poke in the baby's nappy. The child, not being old enough to have any concern for the wealth on which he was sitting, performed his normal functions as only a healthy baby could. The weight of mother nature's "load" and that of the heavy gold poke exposed all to Kate and the hapless constable who had lifted the baby in admiration.

Today, as time for departure drew near, confusion and excitement took over the station. The engine began to build up a head of steam, puffing billows into the autumn air. Leo came to bid his

HP45735

The *Princess Sophia* laiden with troops. (B.C. Archives and Records Service)

aunt good-bye, surrounded by friends who had come to see him off: Bob Lowe, Don Muirhead, his school friends and his two brothers, who anticipated their own departure in the years ahead. Jerry Quinlan's "All Aboard!" interrupted the farewells. With only a few seconds to say good-bye, Kate, in an uncharacteristic gesture, pulled Leo towards her and held him for an instant. She covered his boyish hands with her large strong ones and only reluctantly allowed him to pull away.

The whistles blasted long and sharp as the train began to jerk forward. With slow steps, Kate returned to the station to write up her day's report, while the image of Leo filled her thoughts. A terrible heaviness and sadness came over her.

The White Pass and Yukon Railway had become the territory's life line to the outside since it had been completed in 1900. All normal life revolved around the coming and going of the train, especially after the steamers stopped during the winter. The south-bound train, filled to capacity with passengers and freight, trundled along the narrow-gauge track down the mountains. The breath-taking scenery of the trip from the summit to Skagway was lost on Leo, absorbed as he was in the friends, acquaintances and strangers sharing his adventure on the train. He joined a group of boatmen at the back of the coach, and only the disapproving eye of Jerry Quinlan prevented him from having a swig from the flask they offered him. Excitement heightened to euphoria as the train rumbled into Skagway and to the waiting steamer. It was a gay scene as the *Princes Sophia* bobbed and curtsied in the swelling waters, greeting her boarding passengers. Many of these had known months, even years of loneliness in the far north, and their trip south to the outside was a dramatic event. The were heading to the bright lights, the modern hotels, the motor cars and the moving picture shows.

Earlier in October, a number of men from Alaska had joined the American army and had sailed from Skagway. Their families now boarded the steamer to join them. Old prospectors, businessmen, women and children, a few belated operators from the scattered Army Signal Corps, scores of miners and crews from the last river boats to sail down the Yukon River that year swelled the passenger list of the *Princess Sophia* to 289 souls. At 10 p.m. sharp on October 23, the *Princess Sophia* left Skagway for her return voyage to Prince Rupert, Vancouver and Victoria. She carried very little cargo, but she boasted a full complement of officers and a crew of 61, commanded by Captain John Locke. Captain Locke was an experienced officer, familiar with the difficult waters of the Lynn Canal, but, while Leo and the other passengers explored their new surroundings, the Captain and his officers cautiously watched the barometer dropping. When the steamer was four hours out of port, the wind suddenly came up. Captain Locke was not unduly concerned, as he had navigated these temperamental waters many times before, but, when the wind began to blow in gusts of snow and sleet, he put the crew on full alert. The passengers ignored the raging wind outside and enjoyed the comforts of the plush dining halls and cabins.

Captain Locke expected the storm to subside as usual as they proceeded south, but he became alarmed when the storm increased in its ferocity. As the vessel inched its way down the

Lynn Canal, he was forced to use the blasting whistles to locate the invisible shores on either side. Suddenly, without warning, the mighty steamer gave a jarring shudder. The bow lifted high in the air, and the glorious 2,320-ton steamer went aground on Vanderbilt Reef. The impact threw passengers out of their beds and off their chairs to tumble in hysterics to the open decks. Captain Locke reassured them over the loudspeakers that they were in no danger, and that there was no need for panic or alarm. He had radioed to Vancouver, and the *Princess Sophia's* sister ship, the *Princess Alice*, was on her way to rescue them. Vanderbilt Reef, a shipping hazard well known to experienced sailors along the Alaskan coast, was located latitude 58:35:20 north, longitude 135:00:30 west. Captain Locke couldn't explain how they had drifted a mile and a quarter off course.

Captain Locke's distress signal brought immediate reaction as several small vessels in the area rushed to his assistance. The Lighthouse Tender *Cedar* arrived first, and when the weather conditions cleared somewhat, her captain, John W. Leadbetter, urged Captain Locke to begin to transfer some of his passengers to the smaller boats standing by. Every craft in the area had rushed to the assistance of the *Princess Sophia*, and she was surrounded by a flotilla of vessels of every description. Captain Locke decided against following Leadbetter's advice, convinced that there was no immediate threat. He was more worried about the injuries he believed would befall passengers being evacuated to the smaller boats. The crews of these boats could do nothing but sit and helplessly watch the steamer perched precariously on her rocky throne, her inhabitants waving mournfully to those who waited to assist them. The rough seas and high winds continued through the next day and into the late afternoon. At 4:45 p.m. the log books of the other boats recorded that the wind freshened again. Captain Locke sent a wireless message to the *Cedar* requesting help, but by this time the wind and seas were so high it was impossible to get the passengers off the liner. The captains agreed that the smaller vessels would stand alongside and await the arrival of the *Princess Alice*. They would try to move everyone off the stricken ship at daylight.

The winds did not subside when daylight came but continued with relentless fury. One by one, the rising wind forced the smaller vessels to head for the security of the shore, which was only a short distance away but invisible because of the blinding snow storm. When the darkness of the second evening descended upon them, even the bravest fled to shore, while every captain kept a constant radio watch for messages from the disabled *Princess Sophia.* None came during the night, so they waited for the light of day to begin their rescue attempt again. In the early morning, the winds subsided, and at the first hint of dawn the *Cedar* returned to the *Princess Sophia.* When the ship drew near Vanderbilt Reef, the crew could hardly believe their eyes — the *Princess Sophia* had disappeared. Only her fore topmast breaking the surface of the water marked where she had gone down.

A letter found on the body of one of the passengers told the tale as it was experienced from the deck of the *Princess Sophia.* John Maskell was en route to Vancouver on his way home to marry his sweetheart, Dorothy Burgess, of Manchester, England. Two months after the sinking of the vessel, the authorities sent Dorothy the letter her fiancé had written to her in the last hours of his life. As well as his last will and testament, this letter records Maskell's matter-of-fact acceptance of what fate had in store for him and his companions on the elegant steamer.

> Coast of Alaska
> S.S. Princess Sophia.
> 24th Oct. 1918.
>
> My Own dear Sweetheart, —
>
> I am writing this dear girl while the boat is in grave danger. We struck a rock last night which threw many from their berths, women rushed out in their night attire, some were crying, some too weak to move, but the lifeboats were soon swung out in all readiness, but owing to the storm would be madness to launch until there was hope for the ship, surrounding ships were notified by wireless and in three hours the first steamer came, but cannot get near owing to the storm raging and the reef which we are on. When the tide went down two thirds of the boat was high and dry.

> We are expecting the lights to go out any minute also the fires. The boat might go to pieces for the force of the waves are terrible, making awful noises on the side of the boat which has quite a list to port. No one is allowed to sleep, but believe me dear Dorrie it might have been much worse. Just here there is another big steamer coming. We struck the reef in a terrible snow storm. There is a life buoy near marking the danger but the Captain was to port instead [of] to starboard of buoy. I made my will this morning leaving everything to you my own true love and I want you to give £100 to my dear mother, £100 to my dear father, £100 to dear wee Jack and the balance of my estate (about £300) to you Dorrie dear. The Eagle Lodge will take care of my remains.
>
> Your loving Jack.

The small vessels standing by searched frantically along the reefs and up and down the shore line in the early grey light, hoping desperately to pick up survivors. Their desperate search led them only to four capsized lifeboats rising and falling in the choppy waters of the Lynn Canal. Captain Leadbetter had no recourse but to send the following telegram to the authorities:

> Princess Sophia driven across Vanderbilt Reef. No survivors. Two hundred and eighty nine passengers, sixty one crew. Everything possible was done. Terrible weather prevailed.

The small boats returned to search and search again, hoping that some survivors would be found. Later that day, Captain Leadbetter sent the message that ended all hope:

> No sign of life. No hope for survivors.

Every wireless operator in the area picked up the transmission from the *Cedar*, and word of the disaster spread like wildfire. The message was unbelievable, and everyone thought there must be some mistake. Early on the morning after the *Princess*

Sophia sank, a coded message similar to the one sent by Captain Leadbetter was received by Jim Young, the Whitehorse telegraph operator. Incredulous, Jim asked to have it repeated, but the second message transmitted the same awful news as the first: "Princess Sophia sunk with all hands." Jim was stunned, not only with the magnitude of the message, but by his own personal grief. His brother had been aboard the steamer. Jim bolted out the front door into the street, nearly knocking Bob Lowe off his feet.

"My God, Bob, there has been a terrible disaster." Unable to find the words to tell the story, Jim thrust the message into Bob's hands. The fire bell woke Whitehorse and brought the citizens rushing to the centre of town, where the North West Mounted Police duty officer told them the horrific news. The small community stood in stunned silence around him. Jim spent the next 24 hours glued to the telegraph key, transmitting and receiving messages about the disaster. He asked question after question, but all the answers were the same: "Regret there were no survivors." Not a family in Whitehorse remained untouched by the tragedy. Charlie Cousins lost his wife, as did Danny Gillis and Bill Carr. Bill O'Brien had taken his wife and five children outside for a visit; all seven perished. For Kate there was only silence. She remained in a state of shock for days. The loss of her beloved Leo and so many of her friends and neighbours struck her a heavy blow. She could not have loved Leo more if he had been her natural son. She had been associated intimately with many of the other victims, she had worked with them and talked with them daily for years and she had wished them all *bon voyage*. Now not one remained. With her mourning friends and neighbours, she could scarcely come to terms with so many senseless deaths.

The search for bodies from the *Princess Sophia* continued at a painful pace. Each day, word was received that more bodies had been found. At intervals word would filter in that a child's body, or the body of an unidentified male, or someone else had surfaced or washed up on shore. The agony dragged on and on. Until the body had been found and identified, people could not believe that a loved one was actually dead. Like many others, Kate tormented herself. Perhaps it was all a mistake; maybe Leo had missed the boat; he was a good swimmer, and maybe he had reached shore. She felt responsible for Leo's death; she should never have let him go. This self-persecution went around and around in her mind. She could not stand the waiting and asked the customs inspector for a leave of absence from her job. At least by taking some action she could keep herself busy as, over and over, boats went out to search for bodies. After a few days, she had given up hope of finding Leo alive, and now she prayed that she could have his body to give him a Christian burial.

Ironically, it was the *Tees*, the steamer on which so many had come to the Yukon in the first place, that the B.C. Salvage Company sent to Vanderbilt Reef to search for the wreck of the *Princess Sophia* and try to find out why she sank. The crew of the *Tees* set off a few men in a small gas-powered boat to drag the site of the wreck with a 28-pound lead. This small boat passed slowly back and forth at right angles to the keel of the *Princess Sophia*, dragging the lead behind the boat. By recording where the weight touched bottom and where it touched the sunken steamer, they could tell just where the *Princess Sophia* lay. Every twenty feet or so, they made another pass across the steamer. They were reading eight fathoms of water over the *Princess Sophia's* decks every time they passed over her, when suddenly the lead dropped to seventeen fathoms without touching the wreck. Beyond that point, they obtained 35 fathoms over an ooze bottom. The salvagers concluded that the vessel had broken in two about seventy feet behind the foremast and that the after part of it had sunk into deep water.

Each day increased the anguish as Kate and the other despondent survivors waited for word from the searchers. They clung to every morsel of news, every scrap of evidence, in hopes that it would bring them some message of comfort or at least some answers. But by the first week in November the onset of winter slowed the search, and finally the salvagers' work became impossible. The ship's agent in Skagway notified the searchers on the *Tees* that the Wells Fargo Express Company had shipped a safe containing bullion worth $62,000 on the *Princess Sophia*, but the deplorable weather forced the *Tees* to retreat to Juneau. Valiantly, the *Tees* returned to the wreck once more, this time carrying divers and a plan of the ship showing the location of the safe. As the divers began their search, a message from the postmaster in Dawson said that four mail bags had been aboard, weighing 300 pounds and containing $70,000 in gold. On their second attempt, the divers managed to find the body of George Paddock and the Wells Fargo safe. The current was so strong and conditions so hazardous that once more the *Tees* had to abandon its efforts. A few days later, the *Tees* made a third attempt to uncover the secrets of the reluctant *Princess Sophia*. This time, the divers found the mail bags lying within four feet of the break in the deck. Beyond this point, they could see nothing of the ill-fated steamer. Bad weather at last forced the captain of the *Tees* to abandon his efforts until summer. All told, 24 search boats had recovered 179 bodies, but Leo's was not among them.

Almost three weeks after the disaster, the *Princess Alice* brought into Vancouver a cargo consisting of the bodies that had been recovered from the *Princess Sophia*. The story of the return of the *Princess Alice* was relegated to the second page; the front page headline read: "The War Is Over." Those who had to come to the docks to claim the bodies of their loved ones did not find it easy to share the jubilation that millions around the world took in this wonderful news. A young reporter at dockside captured this heartrending drama.

> In the half light of the docking shed a rough and ready longshoreman with tears blurring his eyes cradled the little white casket of Baby O'Brien in his arms before setting it on the short draped bier.

The Kaiser's capitulation and the end of the war brought little joy to the Whitehorse survivors. The day they had all prayed for came and went and they could not rejoice; the community was shrouded in black, not least for Bill O'Brien's baby.

Each person lost on the *Princess Sophia* had a story to tell, but the full impact of the disaster was never fully appreciated anywhere except in the northern communities that had suffered such terrible losses. After the inquiry into the sinking of the *Princess Sophia* in January, February and March of 1919, a court stenographer tried to put into words his feelings about a disaster that seemed to him beyond human comprehension. He wrote to the Minister of Fisheries:

> There never was and never could be, one would think, a tragedy of the sea more poignant and intense in its nature than this of the "Sophia." The public speaking generally recognised it was an "accident"; but yet nevertheless the Government decided (as did the USA Government) that a most searching inquiry should be held to discover if perchance blame or responsibility might be fixed. They knew — and the public knew — the impossibility of doing more: all those lives had gone beyond recall.

Politics and Parties

The last two weeks in Juneau were bitterly cold as Kate waited for the steamer *Tees* to return from its final attempt to salvage the *Princess Sophia.* When it arrived, it brought the Dawson mail bags and the Wells Fargo safe containing gold, but the divers had found only two bodies. There was no trace of Leo. The captain of the *Tees* repeated his story as he tried to console Kate. The winter weather made conditions in the Lynn Canal hopeless, and he doubted if any more bodies would be found until spring. He urged Kate to return home and try to put the disaster behind her, knowing in his own heart just how difficult that would be. She had always been a pillar of strength against adversity, but this was beyond her endurance. Her final thread of hope tormented her.

Despondent, she returned home, but she found that she could not settle down. Kate knew it was time to leave her beloved Whitehorse. Reluctantly, the customs inspector at the Royal North West Mounted Police detachment accepted her decision to retire. He knew, and Kate knew, that the position of female gold inspector would be abolished when she left, and an epoch would end. Large regulated companies now did the gold mining in the area, taking away the opportunities for smuggling that had made Kate's job so important. Not only was her life changing, but the world was changing all around her, and she had to face up to reality and move on. She must leave the memories behind. When she bundled Johnny and Charlie onto the train for the final time, she did not dare allow herself to look back at the small circle of friends who stood on the platform. They waved bravely as the train pulled out of the station, wondering what the town would be like without the woman who had become so much a part of it. For Kate, the trip to Skagway remained a blur, shrouded behind a veil of tears. She knew she would never return to the land she loved so much.

A group of survivors of those who had lost their lives on the *Princess Sophia* banded together to launch a legal battle against the Canadian Pacific Railway and the governments of Canada and the United States, claiming that the *Princess Sophia* had gone aground because of negligence. Kate, like some of the others, also initiated a personal lawsuit against the United States and Canadian governments, declaring that the loss of her nephew caused grave financial hardship. The Canadian government ordered a public inquiry into the shipping disaster, and Kate felt compelled to attend the hearings that were held in Victoria and Vancouver during the first three months of 1919. Sitting in the courtroom during the long hours of testimony only added to her grief. There seemed to be no answers, no human reason why the luxury liner had strayed so far off course and broken in two on Vanderbilt Reef. Time was really the only medicine for the bereaved families, but for Kate it was also a time to assess her life and contemplate her future.

A letter from her dear friend Frank Mobley offering her a job provided the chance she had prayed for, and she accepted his offer without hesitation. Frank was the newly elected Liberal member for Atlin, and he wanted her to be the Commission Agent in the mining town of Stewart, British Columbia, at the southern end of his district. Frank's letter overflowed with enthusiasm for the future of mining in the area. Deposits of gold, silver, lead and zinc had been found near Stewart, and investors and mining companies were showing a great interest in the potential wealth. Canada had come out of the 1903 Alaska-Canada boundary settlement the loser; the coast of northern British Columbia had been split off and given to the United States, and now it formed the Alaska panhandle. The Portland Canal, an extension of Portland Inlet, marked the southern end of the panhandle. Stewart, at the head of the Portland Canal and a mile and half from the American border, nestled at the base of the Coast Mountains, where the Bear River emptied into the canal. The village of Hyder, Alaska, was just across the boundary line, and the two communities shared their lives and the wealth that surrounded them. Although the population of Stewart had dropped to 17 during the War from a high of 10,000 in the first decade of the century, everyone who now came pouring in believed it would be the next northern Mecca.

Kate arrived in Stewart on the steamer *Prince Rupert* on October 3, 1919. Just as in the old days in Glenora, the arrival of the steamer was an exciting event for the community because it brought in mail, supplies, news, government officials and mining experts. The steamer also delivered new residents to the growing town. Far from being a stranger, Kate said, she felt as if she had come home. She was back in the northern bush, with the mountains surrounding her. Over the years, she had met most of the men and women in Stewart. Some were, like herself, pioneers of the Teslin Trail, and others had come down from Whitehorse at the first word of new gold finds. Kate was not surprised in the least to learn that Dominic Burns had opened a butcher shop in town. His shamrock sign waved a greeting as she walked down the main street. Everywhere she went, she was welcomed with a hearty hello.

She would never forget her first night at the King Edward Hotel. What a reunion! Frank Mobley arrived, accompanied by Billy Orr and Guy Lawrence. Guy had grown into a tall, handsome young man, mature for his years. He had served in Europe during the war, and now he felt grateful to be home again. They reminisced over the early days in Glenora, when Guy had supplied Kate's first restaurant with fish. Now he was following in his father's footsteps; he operated the Stewart telegraph office. Old friends and new acquaintances kept dropping by the King Edward to welcome Kate to her new home, until the evening turned into a party. It was just the tonic Kate needed to help her set herself on a steady course again.

Kate settled into her new position as Commission Agent, and once again, she joined all the social organizations. A "Hard Times Dance" sponsored by the town firemen was a good excuse to retrieve her old trail clothes from her trunk. She washed and pressed the worn riding skirt, put patches on places that needed attention, and added material here and there so that her large body would fit into her former self. With a bit of buckram and a new sprig of artificial flowers, her "cow-breaker hat" was almost as good as new. Dressed for the dance, she turned in the mirror and saw in her reflection all the places she had been in those clothes that had served her so well. As soon as she and Billy Orr entered the brightly-lighted hall, the others drew them into the dance. The men were decked out in their "old diggin'

Kate's home in Stewart, from a postcard on the back of which she wrote, "This is our place and I am waiting to rent it. We live in the back." (Walter Ryan)

clothes," while the women had donned their worn ginghams and linsey-woolseys. They danced to the music and followed the calls of Charlie Lake, who perched on a high straight chair and sang out to everyone to swing their partners to the "Lady of the Lake." Mrs. Al Harris kept her eagle eye on the punch bowl, making certain no good-hearted fellow added anything but the purest fruit juice to the contents. Then the moment of truth arrived: the awarding of the prizes for the best costumes. Kate and Billy, judged the most original and authentic, took first prize. They promenaded around the dance floor to music of their friends' cheers. As she accepted the prize, Kate told her friends gathered around her how ironic it seemed to win a prize for the same outfit that was her normal dress twenty years before. It seemed doubly humorous that her famous "cow-breaker hat" still proved to be her good luck charm. She guessed she would start wearing it again.

The weekly dances became more than a popular local event, they became famous. Word of the colourful Stewart dances spread through the interior and as far away as Vancouver. The Citizens' Association received a formal request from the Gaumont *Weekly* for a delegation to attend for the purpose of making a modern movie of the gay social event. The news that a movie was about to be made in Stewart turned the town into a beehive. Fire Chief Bill Rogers put a notice in the weekly Stewart *News* announcing that the cooperation of everyone in town would be needed. All the citizens must do their part by putting on their "diggin' clothes," or finding some other proper costume of the pioneer days. The film crew and the visitors they attracted created a commotion in the small town. Pioneers for miles around arrived dressed in their finest old prospecting clothes, and those who had not complied with the Fire Chief's edict were fined heavily on the spot. Ken Suratt, from the Gaumont *Weekly*, took charge of filming the moving picture. He told the editor of the Stewart *News* that he felt honoured to have the opportunity of witnessing a real northern dance, so unique and picturesque, with everyone dressed in colourful pioneer clothes. Suratt was most impressed by the North West Mounted Police, who, in their old-fashioned scarlet tunics, added to the spectacle .

Once again, the awarding of the prizes was the highlight of the evening, the waltz prize going this time to Tom Taylor and Mrs. Pete Murphy. Charlie Riley worked feverishly on the piano to keep up to the demands of the dancers. When the evening finally came to a close, everyone agreed — there had never been an event to compare with this one in the entire history of Stewart.

Following the excitement of movie-making, Kate's life took on a regular pattern as she settled into her job. The position gave her a new perspective on business, and her experience with mining gave her the confidence she needed to do well in her work. The position also offered an opportunity to travel to Vancouver and Victoria to promote the development of the mining industry. In an interview published in the *Daily Colonist*, Kate announced a great future for the Premier Mine and the great potential it offered to investors in Stewart and Hyder.

"No mine," Kate predicted, "will be equal to the Premier Mine which will surely become the greatest mining centre in the world . . . The Stewart Camp is my eighth sojourn, but I'm not done for yet. The northern settlement possesses 500 inhabitants, but I'm confident that in twelve months the place will contain three times as many citizens. . . . The assistance of the government in the construction of a tram will make it possible for the ore to be shipped at great savings in cost. It should be pointed out," she added, "that a great amount of exporting necessary goods takes place from Vancouver. In exchange for what the north receives, we produce a great deal of wealth for the province."

Kate concluded her interview by telling the reporter that she was in town on personal as well as government business. She wanted investors to look at what the north had to offer.

In Stewart, Kate was much closer to Vancouver than she had been in Whitehorse, and so she made frequent trips south. Content with her life, she purchased the Herb Anderson place near the Lake and Green warehouse in Hyder, and her work and her social activities kept her constantly on the go. But then, once again, her life was altered. The unexpected death of her friend Frank Mobley left her bereaved, but also it put her job, a political appointment, in question. Because of Frank's death, the Atlin seat was vacant and a by-election was imminent. The Liberal Association held meetings to discuss a potential candidate, and much to Kate's surprise, her name kept being suggested. At first, she scoffed at the idea, but it became clear that certain members of the executive were not only serious, but determined that she should be selected. T. Duff Pattulo, the former mayor of Prince Rupert and now the member for the Prince Rupert district, took over the duties of the Atlin district until the by-election. Stewart buzzed with rumours when the Association asked him to come to town for a most important meeting. With Pattulo as their spokesman, a delegation from the Liberal Association asked Kate formally if she would consider running as the Liberal candidate. She could hardly refuse a formal request from such an important and credible politician as Duff Pattulo, but Kate said she would just have to think about it. The offer tempted her, but she was not convinced that she wanted the job.

The men argued that the country needed more women; Mary Ellen Smith's victory in the previous election had laid the ground

Kate at the time of her proposed candidacy for the Atlin district. (KMK)

work for women candidates; and, they persisted, hadn't Kate herself worked to gain women the right to vote in elections? Why not run in them also? The logic of Kate's nomination made a lot of sense to the politicians in Stewart, and her experience and reputation in the mining and business community would guarantee her a lot of support. They were confident that, if she would accept the nomination, she would be elected. Kate could not put the idea away lightly. There were many personal reasons why she should forget the challenge, but she had never faced life that way and was not about to start doing so now. On the other hand, she was 53 years old, hardly a time in life to consider a new career, let alone one in politics. But the argument remained: there was a great need for a woman's voice to be heard in government. She herself had many dreams of changes she would like the government to make, and the voices of prospectors and miners speaking up for their rights needed to be heard in Victoria.

While Kate Ryan considered her possible future in politics, Mary Ellen Smith bravely fought for the reforms and election promises she had made to the women of British Columbia. The Liberal government finally accepted Mrs. Smith's proposals for a minimum wage for women, and it also debated the idea of mothers' pensions. The Attorney General, E. Farrier, drafted the minimum wage bill, and Mrs. Smith provided the force to drive it through the British Columbia Legislature. The new Minimum Wage Act called for an unpaid administrative board of three, of which at least one should be a woman. This was the first such board instituted in Canada, and its establishment told the women of the province that the Liberal government was dedicated to reform and concerned about their welfare. Kate knew all about this movement, and deeply desired to take part in the reform, but she doubted that she could take part in the rapid changes occurring in the modern age of the 1920's.

The executive of the Stewart Liberal Association urged Kate to accept the nomination, but she told them to wait until the by-election was actually called. Her possible candidacy caused an unusual amount of speculation; newspapers began to seek information, and items about her appeared in papers in Vancouver and Seattle, and even as far away as Ottawa and New Brunswick. Headlines in the New Brunswick papers read, "Woman Sourdough Seeks to Enter B.C. Legislature." "Pioneer Yukon Woman May Contest Atlin Seat," proclaimed the Vancouver paper. Reporters took the opportunity to review Kate's life in the north, repeating stories of her accomplishments and showering her with accolades for her heroic deeds. On a business trip to Vancouver, she was the darling of the newspapers, as reporters rushed to interview the famous lady. The wire services picked up the stories, and reprints appeared in Whitehorse, Edmonton, Calgary and most of the big cities in the east. The headlines and subheads varied: "Woman Suggested to Contest the Atlin Seat," "Pioneer Woman May Seek Election — Heroine of the Yukon Stampede May Seek Liberal Nomination." Visiting Seattle, she received the same attention, as the papers relived the trek of '98.

The Seattle *Post-Intelligencer* reported, "Sergeant Kate is In Town," and continued,

> Miss Katherine Ryan, the only woman who was ever made a member of the Royal North West Mounted Police, famous throughout Canada, arrived in Seattle on the *Princess Charlotte.* Miss Ryan is the only woman in the world who has served as a gold commissioner . . . Miss Ryan left the government service to enter the mercantile business in Stewart, B.C., located at the head of the Portland Canal. She is young in years and appearance. Her experience in the north and her knowledge of northern conditions led friends to urge her become a candidate for the provincial election.

After spending five weeks outside as the cynosure of the press, business people, salesmen and friends, Kate found coming home more worthwhile than ever. Grateful for the security of the Stewart docks and the mountains behind them, she realized that the south stifled her and the hectic bustle of city life overwhelmed her. Her only salvation was the knowledge that she could escape back to the northern bush. Perhaps it was all the public attention that finally helped Kate to make up her mind about the Liberal nomination. Not only could she not face presenting herself as a politician, but the title "Klondike Kate" had reappeared, and she did not want to be associated with the well-publicized dance-hall floozy ever again. No matter how many years had passed, the connection kept recurring. As far as she could remember, she had hardly seen the inside of the notorious dance halls of the north, and she had never even made it to Dawson. After thinking over the problem long and hard, she gave the executive her decision.

"I deeply respect the offer of the Association," she said, "but, gentlemen, it is not the life for me. I could not be content in political life. I am too much a part of the great outdoors to be confined to brick walls. I need Mother Nature around me. I do thank you for the honour but I must decline your offer."

Her decision made, Kate stepped aside for H.E. (Bert) Kerrigan, who was duly elected as the new Liberal representative for the Atlin district. Meanwhile, Kate went about her business, silently wondering if she could have won the election and done the job in Victoria. Christmas came as it did every year. Kate loved Christmas, and as always, she went out of her way to entertain and make special thoughtful gifts for her friends. There was a new mission priest in Stewart, and Kate was pleased to have the Christmas Mass offered for Leo, whom she still remembered in her every prayer. Her friend Billy Orr, always full of fun and good humour, stopped to show her his new claim to fame: his own Christmas story printed in the Stewart *News*. He had told a reporter a favourite joke about a neighbour with a reputation for being close with his money.

"My Scottish neighbour is so tight," Billy's story went, "that he went outside and fired a gun shot up into the air. He came back inside and told his wife and children Santa had just committed suicide so there would be no presents."

In spite of Billy's story, Santa did come, and so did New Year's Eve and the annual ball sponsored by the Citizens' Association. Kate took charge of all the decorations, and what better person than Billy to see to the impersonation of Father Time. The poor fellow, disguised as 1920, made a tour of the dance floor, bedraggled and weather-worn. To a lugubrious tune, he dragged himself out of the hall, and was replaced at once by a smart young man, in the shape of Guy Lawrence, proudly portraying the New Year, 1921. Cheers went up all round as the people of Stewart danced the New Year in.

The new year brought the promised economic prosperity to the Atlin district. The mines continued to pay good dividends to the shareholders, and work was abundant as the whole area enjoyed the boom. Stewart stepped into the modern age when a local company offered to supply the growing town and vicinity with electric power, water and telephone service. The Liberal Association elected a new executive, including Kate as a director, and they sent a telegram to the newly elected member, Bert Kerrigan, inviting him to pay a spring visit to Stewart. At the annual meeting of the Citizens' Association, the executive recommended a motion that "a delegation appointed by the chair wait on Miss Kate Ryan with a view to get her to join the Association."

Kate accepted the invitation and became the first woman to sit on the board of directors of the Stewart Citizens' Association.

That spring, Kate made a trip to Vancouver once again to attend the court hearings on her *Princess Sophia* lawsuit. Two and a half years after the disaster, the battle and the agony continued for Kate and the other families, who still received neither answers nor settlement of their claims. After such a long trial, the outcome disappointed the dependents of the *Princess Sophia* victims; the court awarded them no compensation for the loss of their loved ones. The verdict was not surprising, since the official inquiry into the wreck had found the owners of the ship and the governments of Canada and the United States blameless. Even so, the defeat added to the feeling of hopelessness the disaster had inflicted on everyone it had touched.

Bert Kerrigan had asked Kate to attend the sitting of the Provincial Legislature while she was south. Mary Ellen Smith acted as her hostess. Kate was delighted to see the workings of the provincial capital, but, although she was very impressed indeed, she confessed to her friends that she knew now she had made the right decision. She was not cut out to be a politician.

When she came back to Stewart, she brought her cousin Bun Hillman who had come from Minneapolis to work at the Premier Mine. The abundant work in the mines and the excellent wages led many new families into the area. The Stewart paper, now called the Portland Canal *News* carried all the news, world and local, and the editor used the paper to tell funny stories in the jargon of the day. "The news circulation is limited to one million, Pilgrim, if you are not on the list, get on at once as the circulation is jumping towards that mark," he would say. Another day, he ran as his *bon mot* , "In the police court in Vancouver last Friday, 193 cases were on the docket. The same day the docket at Stewart was blank. All of which goes to prove that Stewart citizens are law abiding." Another week, he joked, "Thomas Fournier, considered the original Poleon Doret in Rex Beache's book, 'The Barrier,' is now employed on one of the Premier's tractors." His vital statistics listed seven births, four deaths and two marriages in Stewart that year, certainly a record for a booming town.

The Citizens' Association at last established a small hospital in

The photo of Kate which appeared with the 1922 *Maclean's* article by William Lewis Edmunds.

Stewart, and Kate became the first nursing matron, once again returning to her first career. During that same summer of 1922, William Lewis Edmunds interviewed Kate for an article he was writing. Edmunds spent the summer touring the northern Yukon and the Alaska Panhandle, seeking out those who were involved in the Gold Rush of '98. Hearing that Kate lived in Stewart, he travelled in on the supply boat *Princess Alice* early in the summer. Kate reluctantly agreed to the interview, but after he left she forgot about it until the December issue of *Maclean's Magazine* arrived. To her amazement, one of the issue's most important features was Edmunds's story about her life. Edmunds had titled the story, "The Woman Called Klondike Kate," and the subhead made the theme of the story clear: "One of the First Few Women To Enter the Klondike in the Trying Years of '98. A Hint of the Varied Experiences In Her Eventful Life."

"Among the human element that ventured into the Klondike during the placer gold mining boom of nearly a quarter of a century ago," he began, "the one that was destined to become the most outstanding and best know figure, was a woman — Kate Ryan, or, as the mining fraternity dubbed her, 'Klondike Kate.' " Edmunds outlined the life and journey of Kate into the Yukon in 1898, and he gave her own account of the life she had shared with the other pioneers during the gold rush. "For her courage," he said, "she was outstanding. She feared nothing and there was nowhere in the Klondike wilderness into which she hesitated to mush when whim impelled or necessity demanded."

On his voyage to Stewart, Edmunds had interviewed other pioneers of the north, one of whom told him, " 'Kate Ryan, because of her penchant for helping the other fellow, was everywhere known as the miner's friend. Whenever she heard that some poor devil was lying sick and alone on the trail she'd get to him if she could possibly. I've known her in the winter time mush in with a dog team for a hundred miles and bring a sick fellow out. If ever there was a Good Samaritan in the Klondike, it was Kate Ryan.' "

Edmunds asked Kate why, after she reached Wrangell, Alaska and saw the dangers ahead, she didn't just turn around and go back. "What in the world would have been the use of going back?" Kate answered. "Sure, wouldn't I have only been going over the same ground and seen the things I had already seen? At any rate, I wasn't built for going backwards, when I once step forward I must go ahead."

When Edmunds complemented Kate on her youthful appearance, she quipped, " 'Young woman, eh! Well that's good. Now just for your benefit I'll do for you that which I do for other men who hand me out stuff like that.' Then, whipping off the very broad-brimmed 'cow-breaker' hat she wore and exposing a wealth of snow-white hair sparingly touched with the rich dark auburn that originally crowned her head, she continued,'Tell me, now, is that the hair of a young woman?'" A blast from the steamer whistle abruptly concluded the meeting between the writer and the heroine of the north. Kate stepped lightly down the gang plank to join the men waiting for the steamer to sail. As the *Princess Alice* slipped her ropes and headed out into the Portland Canal, Edmunds could see the tall powerful lady waving her hat, a commanding figure against the mountain backdrop.

Edmunds caught the spirit of Katherine Ryan as no other writer had done. He had taken the time to talk to her, and had listened carefully and not depended on others for fabricated legends. To Kate's embarrassment, his article dwelt on her heroic qualities until it made her "sound like a saint." Although she could not get used to reading stories about her own life, the only really upsetting feature of the *Maclean's* article was Edmunds's revival of the nickname "Klondike Kate."

Kate put the magazine in the bottom of her black bag with the rest of her memories. With Christmas coming again, she had little time to play the heroine. She expected company for the holidays, and there was no end to the work that had to be done.

Late in 1923, after an absence of almost 22 years, Kate and Johnny made preparations to go home to Johnville. By chance and fate, they met Kate's old friend Nellie Tashman in Vancouver, and the three travelled across the continent together. Nellie was en route to New York City, and Kate and John's first stop was to visit James in Minneapolis. From Minneapolis, they carried on to Nora's home in Bangor, Maine, and at last they came home to New Brunswick and the hills of Johnville. Kate's parents had long since passed away. John had married again and now served as the local sheriff. With his wife, he lived in the village of Bath, just behind the station and not far from Gallagher's store. When Kate and young Johnny arrived home, they were met by Charlie, who had just returned from working on a cargo ship in Europe. For the first time since babyhood, the boys were united with their Father. Bob, the baby Kate had taken back to Whitehorse in 1902, and Walter, the baby who remianed in Johnville, joined in the homecoming. The local newspaper dubbed the reunion "When East Meets West." Charlie and Johnny, true northerners that they were, didn't stay long in New Brunswick. Like their aunt, they were not content to be away from the North for very long. New Brunswick was only a place they had come from, not their home.

In Bath and Johnville, the younger generation especially fell into a frenzy of excitement over having the celebrated Miss Ryan in their midst. Years later, Tom Bohan recalled meeting Kate Ryan when he was a child. Every detail of that thrilling event was etched in his memory. He had been sent to the Ryan household on an errand, and when the famous Kate herself answered the door, he nearly fainted.

"When Miss Kate opened the door, I was so shocked I could not utter a word," Tom remembered. "I had heard so many stories about her being a policewoman and a jailer that when she came to the door, I just froze. I couldn't say a word, couldn't

The Ryan homestead, Johnville, New Brunswick, 1923.
Pat Ryan (Kate's father) is seated, her brother John (with hat) and his second wife, Annie McGrotty, are standing in the centre and John Jr. is on horseback (KMK)

even tell her who I was. She coaxed me into the house, sat me on a stool, and bribed me with a big molasses cookie while she returned to kneading this great big batch of bread. As I watched her pound that bread my eyes were as big as the cookie thinking about how strong she was."

Tom's imagination soared until he regained himself enough to tell her his name and his errand. His fears evaporated while they chatted and he even managed to ask questions about the Yukon.

"She gave me the parcel for Aunt Catherine — they were school girl friends," Tom recalled, "and I bolted for the door. I ran down the street lickity-split to tell the boys I had just met 'Klondike Kate,' and the stories were all true — she was as strong as a bull!"

Even though he was a little younger than Tom, Clarence Corcoran too remembered meeting Kate the summer she came home. His father, Kate's old friend Henry Corcoran, announced at breakfast that Clarence should put on his Sunday overalls. They were going to town to meet Kate Ryan.

"When Father first greeted her," Clarence said, "he called her 'Klondike Kate.' She was real upset with him and said, 'Henry, if you are truly my friend you will never call me by that name again. After what that other woman has done, I never want to hear that name in my life.' Dad himself was a little upset, but after they got over that they both settled down to have a great visit. They talked about Whitehorse and Johnville, and how things had changed. I was young, so I didn't really pay much attention, but I remember standing beside my father, with my mouth open, recognizing that I was in the presence of a very special lady. Miss Ryan was the first famous person I had ever met in real life, and I knew that she was real important." Smitten by her friendly manner, Clarence added, "I knew that I had met a real hero."

Kate returned to Stewart later that summer, glad to be back in the bush and near the mountains with Johnny and Charlie. The years of hard work had taken their toll on Kate's health, and so, with her dividends from the mines, she purchased a house in Vancouver in which to spend the winter months. The new place on Robson Street was an investment for her retirement, but, more important to her, in Vancouver, as in Stewart, she had a host of friends, relatives and acquaintances. In the city, she kept up her involvement with politics and social organizations. Her ally Mary Ellen Smith had appointed her to the Minimum Wage Board, and she faithfully attended meetings of the Red Cross and the Order of Yukon Pioneers. Much to her delight, the Reverend John Pringle, now Moderator of the Presbyterian Church of Canada, came to Vancouver to officiate at the dedication of a stained glass window installed in Christ Church Anglican Cathedral as a tribute to the men and women of the north who had given their lives during the war in Europe. Once again, the men and women of the trails united in worship under the guidance of John Pringle. The Reverend did not disappoint them, as his words took them back out on the Yukon trails. Eloquently he remembered those of their number lost in the war and those who had lost their lives on the *Princess Sophia*. In blessing the window, he also asked the Creator's blessing on the brave people gathered in the church, for they too had been to battle many times.

After the service, the group gathered for a reception that was one of the most touching events of Kate's life. Once again, she broke bread with John Pringle and her friends from Glenora and Whitehorse, friends with whom she had shared life and death, prosperity and near-starvation. Yet even those whose lives had brought them wealth and fame recognized that their salvation had been in each other and the brotherly love that had united them.

As the years passed, Kate maintained a busy social and business life in Stewart and Vancouver. Her place in Hyder, too, gave her a sense of security and pride. Stewart celebrated Canada's Diamond Jubilee on July 1, 1927, in grand style, with a parade, a picnic and a dance in the evening. The parade, complete with a band, floats and many townspeople dressed in their costumes of bygone years, marched from the schoolyard to the picnic grounds. Woodsmen, prospectors, politicians and Victorian ladies filled the streets, until, after the picnic, the revellers gathered for the dance to celebrate the anniversary of their country and toast their prosperity. Always proud of her Irish ancestry, Kate was well versed in the stories of the old country, but the homeland across the ocean was only a dream world to her. She had travelled Canada from east to west and back again, and she could not imagine that any place else on earth could be as beautiful as where she was. For her, Canada meant her family's freedom from oppression and her own freedom to live in the beauty of the wilderness. She felt a strong sense of pride that she and her country had grown together.

The long days of summer rolled along as the citizens of Stewart enjoyed their prosperity in the warm sun. The Catholic Women's League held a bazaar in August, Father John LeRoy returned to Stewart following a long illness, St. Felix's built an addition onto their small church, and Kate contributed her favourite recipe for white fruit cake to the Anglican women's cook book. Guy Lawrence married Marjorie Brown, and the town shared their joy. Kate made an unscheduled trip outside to be matron of honour for her friend Rosina Wells, who was married in the Presbyterian Church in Vancouver. Johnny, Charlie and Ernie Mustowe went out to the Marmot River to do some work for International Metals.

The children of Stewart named the little stream that ran behind Miss Kate's house Kate Ryan's Brook. When Kate first moved to Stewart, she had formed the habit of walking along the brook whenever she felt the need for mental refreshment. She was not young any more, and she seemed to feel tired all the time. Putting this feeling down to old age creeping up on her, she took another stroll along the stream. The cold water beat almost silently against the shallow banks. The sounds that met her ears were the quiet sounds of nature. The birds seemed to respect her solitude as they watched her pass, deep in reflection on the days gone by and the days to come. Reaching her usual resting place, she sighed out loud as she lowered herself to the rock that waited for her, and she laughed to think that she needed such a solid rock for her large form. It had been a long time since she had allowed herself the luxury of relaxing in the sun. She wondered why she hadn't done it more often. Work, work, always something more to do. Her body ached as she admitted to herself that she was tired, very tired. The quiet of the woods engulfed her as she let her mind wander. She thought of the many friends she had loved over the years, and of Bob, Leo, Johnny and Charlie. Many times, her boys had given her a reason for going on, but they were men now — all but Leo — and looking after themselves. No one tied her to the earth any more, no husband, no one to whom she was obligated. Only God was left. After all her hard work, after the life she had led, maybe God would keep a place for her in heaven.

The afternoon sun was high as the warm rays caressed her into a hazy sleep. Half-dozing, she watched a large raven perform for her in the sky high above her. She soared with him on his majestic flight, up and up to the tops of the trees, over the sparkling rivers and into the mountains. What, she wondered, lay beyond those mountains? What did they hold for her?

Epilogue

Kate Ryan, the "Big Sister" of the north at 4:15 on Saturday morning last, February 20th, reached the end of her last long trail in St. Paul's Hospital, Vancouver, after a lingering illness, the end of which had for some time been anticipated with a sincere sense of sorrow by the communities of Stewart and district, where she has been a resident, with her two nephews, John and Charlie Ryan, since 1919, and where she gave so freely of that great and charitable spirit that endeared her to thousands, and where [for] years no committee was complete, no community organization thought of functioning without her, and where no night was too cold, no distance too great, and no storm too severe to restrain her from going to those who might be sick, injured or in trouble, if she were able to help them.

As a tribute to her great character and the high esteem in which she was held by this entire community, no sooner had the word of her passing been received in Stewart than wires were used freely. The village wired instructions for a wreath to accompany the remains to their last long resting place. The local branch of the Canadian Legion wired similar instructions, and to its Provincial Command to be represented at the funeral services. In this connection Robert McNichol, Provincial Secretary of the Canadian Legion, attended on behalf of the Stewart Branch, and has reported by letter received in town yesterday that in her last hours on this earth, the late Miss Ryan was accorded the honour of an escort of the Royal Canadian Mounted Police. The local Liberal Association of which the deceased was for years an important member, also sent a wreath.

A formal portrait of Kate from the late 1920s (KMK)

> Requiem mass was celebrated at the Holy Rosary Cathedral at 9 a.m. on Tuesday by Rev. Father Nichol. Following the service, the casket was carried to the hearse between the lines of a detachment of the Royal Canadian Mounted Police. A long funeral cortege then proceeded to Ocean View Burial Park where interment took place.
>
> Pallbearers were Messrs. J. Brennan, George Dwyer, Frank J. Burd, D. Burns, Major Z.T. Wood and Inspector C.E. Wilcox of the Mounted Police.

So reported the Stewart *News* on February 26, 1932. In death, Kate was surrounded by those with whom she had shared her life and her adventures. They laid her to rest where she could still see her beloved mountains. Many years later, a Johnville friend asked a stranger to lay flowers on Kate's grave. The spot itself was not hard to find, the stranger replied, but added, "There is no marker, nothing to see. Nobody marked the grave." Perhaps this is what Kate would have wanted. It accords well with her remarks to William Lewis Edmunds, who had asked her why she went to the Klondike. "To tell you the truth," she said, "I never felt at home in the civilization that obtains in our cities and towns. In fact, I hated it. While walking along the streets of a city and gazing upon the paved streets, the concrete sidewalks and the towering buildings, I would say to myself in scorn, 'The work of man, that and nothing else.' So I gradually became more and more obsessed with the desire to live and have my being where things were made by God."

In the late 1920's, magazines and newspapers continued to publish articles about "Klondike Kate." Some gave accurate information, while others confused Katherine Ryan's deeds with those of the dance-hall queen Kitty Rockwell, not without encouragement from Miss Rockwell herself. Only William Lewis Edmunds interviewed Kate to get the real story of her life. Inspired perhaps by his story in *Maclean's*, and certainly by her visit home, the *Carleton Sentinel*, in Woodstock, New Brunswick, carried a long article dramatizing Kate's life as a Yukon pioneer. But Kate paid little attention to these reports. Fate had other adventures in store for her.

The effects of the New York stock market crash in 1929 spread even to the tiny community of Stewart. The repercussions on the mining industry were catastrophic, and along with thousands of others, Kate lost the money she had invested in the mines. After more difficulties, she also lost her place in Hyder. The woman who had devoted her life to the service of others was now reduced to financial hardship. Fortunately, she still had her winter home in Vancouver, and there she spent her last days, ill and poor.

Decades later, the Ryan place in Johnville burned, leaving nothing but a few rocks and boulders from the original foundation as a reminder of the labours of the pioneers who once lived there. The brook still runs behind the old orchard, which has long since grown wild. The fallen apples feed the deer and an occasional bear wandering past in the fall. Few relatives remain who can remember meeting Kate Ryan. Only John Sullivan, a man in his late eighties, can describe the great lady to those who venture to ask, and he still treasures the wedding gift Kate gave to his own mother and father. The younger generation can repeat some of the stories they have heard, but they are confused by the discrepancies between the family version and the accounts in their history books.

But there comes a time when the truth is finally told. The truth is that the original "Klondike Kate" came from the small Irish Community of Johnville, New Brunswick. After getting a taste for adventure in Seattle and Vancouver, she joined the rush to the Yukon in '98. In 1924, a *Carleton Sentinel* reporter extracted from Kate a promise that "some day when life is not so strenuous, and if fortune favours her, she will have her experiences and life story of the Yukon, with its many tragic and humorous sides, written so that Canadians will know for the first time at first hand, just what the trail of '98 meant . . . and whose real life began with that date, in the glorious company of hardy adventurers." Here is Kate's story.

Index

Bibliography

Archives and Museum Collections

National Archives of Canada:

RG18 Vols. 154, 178, 343: Royal Canadian Mounted Police Files, Yukon Division: Law and Order, 1897 - 1919; Letterbooks, Diaries, Local Orders — Upper Yukon 1898; Primrose, Philip Carteret Hill; Sessional Papers: 1898, 1903, 1905, Department of the Interior.

RG18 Vol. 146: Crown Land Survey, Teslin Lake Trail, 1897.

RG42: Transcripts of Hearings and Inquest into the sinking of the *Princess Sophia.*

MG30: Woodside, Henry Joseph: Manuscripts, Diaries, Photos.

Glenbow-Alberta Institute:

Phillip Carteret Hill Primrose: A Historical Sketch

Books

Adney, Tappan. *The Klondike Stampede.* New York: Harper, 1900.

Bennett, Gordon. *Yukon Transportation.* Canadian Historic Sites, No. 19. Ottawa: Parks Canada, 1978.

Berton, Pierre. *Klondike.* Toronto: McLelland and Stewart, 1961.

Coates, Ken and Bill Morrison. *The Sinking of the Princess Sophia.* Don Mills: Oxford, 1990.

Dill, W.S. *The Long Day: Reminiscences of the Yukon.* Ottawa: Graphic, 1926.

Hamilton, Walter R. *The Yukon Story.* Vancouver: Mitchell, 1964.

Jebb, Richard. *Studies in Colonial Nationalism.* London: Arnold, 1905.

Kilfoil, William. *Johnville: The Centennial Story of an Irish Settlement.* Fredericton: privately printed, 1962.

Klinck, Carl F. *Robert Service: A Biography.* New York: Dodd, Mead, 1976.

Lucia, Ellis. *Klondike Kate.* Sausalito, CA: Comstock, 1978.

MacGill, Elsie Gregory. *My Mother the Judge.* Toronto: PMA Books, 1981.

Morrison, David R. *The Politics of the Yukon Territory, 1898-1909.* Toronto: U of Toronto, 1968.

Morton, W.L. *The Canadian Identity.* Toronto: U of Toronto, 1961.

Neering, Rosemary. *Continental Dash: The Russian-American Telegraph.* Ganges, B.C.: Horsdal & Schubart, 1989.

Service, Robert. *Ploughman of the Moon.* New York: Dodd, Mead, 1945; rpt. 1948.

Service, Robert. *Rhymes of a Red Cross Man.* Toronto: Briggs, 1916.

Wright, Allen A. *Prelude to Bonanza: The Discovery and Exploration of the Yukon.* Sidney, B.C.: Gray's, 1976.

Articles, Periodicals and Newspapers

These citations are not always complete because many newspaper and magazine clippings were given to me without full identification.

Alaskan, 5 Jan. 1902.

Alaskan-Yukon Mining Journal, Dec. 1901.

Bangor, Maine *Daily News*, March 1932.

Brown, James McCredie. "The Yukon was Almost a Republic." Vancouver *Province.*

Disher, Arthur L. "The Long March of the Yukon Field Force."

Edmunds, William Lewis. "The Woman Called Klondike Kate." *Maclean's Magazine*, Dec. 1922.

Fenton, Faith. Reports from the Teslin Trail. Toronto *Globe*, July - Oct. 1898.

Glenora *News*, 17 June - 17 Sept. 1898.

Hartland, N.B. *Observer*, 23 Nov. 1924.

Lawrence, Guy. "Forty Years on the Telegraph." *B.C. Digest*, 1964.

Leechman, Douglas. "The Stikine Territory." *Landmarks of History.*
Ottawa *Citizen*, 1 Nov. 1901.
Portland Canal News, 8 Aug. 1919 - 30 March 1928.
San Francisco *Call*, 17 Nov. 1901.
Seattle *Post-Intelligencer*, 22 Nov. 1897.
Skagway *Daily News*, 21 and 22 Oct. 1901.
Stewart, B.C. *Cassiar News*, 30 May 1919 - 1 Aug. 1919.
Stewart, B.C. *News*, 6 Apr. 1928 - Mar. 1932.
Vancouver *Sun*, 1898; 1932.
Victoria *Daily Colonist*, 1919 - 1932.
Victoria *Daily Times*, 8 Sept. 1920; 2 Mar. 1921.
Whitehorse *Star*, 1901 - 1932.
Windsor, John. "Pioneers of British Columbia: The Yukon Field Force." *B.C. Digest*, Vol. 19.
Woodstock, N.B. *Sentinel*, 22 Feb. 1924.